FOREIGN POLICY OF BHUTAN

FOREIGN POLICY OF BHUTAN

Kapileshwar Labh

KALPAZ

ISBN: 978-93-5128-173-3

Price: ₹ 590

First Published, 2016

Published by

Kalpaz Publications
C-30, Satyawati Nagar,
Delhi – 110052
E-mail: kalpaz@hotmail.com
Ph.: 9212142040

Printed at: G. Print Process, Delhi

Cataloging in Publication Data—DK
Courtesy: D.K. Agencies (P) Ltd. <docinfo@dkagencies.com>

Labh, Kapileshwar, author.
Foreign policy of Bhutan / Kapileshwar Labh.
pages cm
Includes bibliographical references.
ISBN 9789351281733

1. Bhutan--Foreign relations. I. Title.

DS492.4.L33 2016 DDC 327.5498 23

Contents

Preface

The present work is the first systemic study of the foreign policy of Bhutan. There are 10 chapters of this study. Chapter 1 is an introductory chapter which deals briefly with Bhutan's history and its political development. Chapter 2 comprises a brief study of the conceptual framework of foreign policy.

Bhutan's geographical location is a significant factor which has determined its foreign policy. Chapter 3 includes the study of the impact of this factor on Bhutan's foreign policy. Bhutan is a small country. By and large, all small countries have similar approach to their foreign policies. Chapter 4 includes an analysis of foreign policies of small states. International environment and domestic milieu are major determinants of foreign policy. Chapter 5 comprises the study of influences of these factors on Bhutan's foreign policy. Chapter 6 has included the study of changes and continuity in Bhutan's regional policy, i.e., policy towards India, Nepal, Bangladesh, and regional Groups, viz., SAARC and BIMSTEC.

Chapter 7 comprises the analysis of Bhutan's world view and its role in the U.N. and the Non-aligned Movement. In Chapter 8, an attempt has been made to study not only the traditional pattern of Bhutan's foreign economic policy but also recent trends in its policy towards its foreign aid and trade. Chapter 9 contains the study of Bhutan's policy towards China and India. Chapter 10 includes the study of the role of the Monarchy, the National

Assembly, the Royal Advisory Council, the Ministry of Foreign Affairs and pressure groups in Bhutan's foreign policy decision-making process. Chapter 11 comprises the retrospect and prospects of Bhutan's foreign policy.

The study is largely based on the Royal Government of Bhutan's documents and publications. I have also drawn on Kuensel, the national newspaper of Bhutan.

I am thankful to the Indian Council of Social Science Research for a grant which enabled me to undertake my field-trip to Bhutan.

I am also thankful to the Royal Government of Bhutan especially His Majesty King Jigme SingyeWangchuck, late Lyonpo Dawa Tsering, Lyonpo Dago Tshering, Lyonpo C. Dorji, Lyonpo Jigmi Y.Thinley, Lyonpo Yeshey Zimba and Lyonpo Sonam T. Rabgye for granting me audience and responding to my questions on their country's foreign policy, and for allowing me to collect source material in Bhutan for my research work.

I am grateful to Professor Bimal Prasad, former Dean, School of International Studies, Jawaharlal Nehru University, New Delhi, Ambassador to Nepal, and Editor of Selected Works of Jayaprakash Narayan, for his inspiration and encouragement. I am also thankful to my colleagues at the South Asian Studies Division, for their valuable suggestions. Finally, I thank the staff of Jawaharlal Nehru University Library, and the staff of Nehru Memorial Museum and Library, Teen Murti House, New Delhi, for helping me in doing my research work.

Abbreviations

ADB	:	Asian Development Bank
BCCI	:	Bhutan Chamber of Commerce and Industries
BPP	:	Bhutan People's Party
BTF	:	Bhutan Trust Fund
ESCAF	:	Economic and Social Commission for Asia and the Pacific
EEC	:	European Economic Committee
FAO	:	Food and Agricultural Organisation
GOI	:	Government of India
IDA	:	International Development Association
IFAD	:	International Fund for Agricultural Development
IMTRAT	:	Indian Military Training Team
JICA	:	Japan International Cooperation Agency
KCIE	:	Knight Commander of Indian Empire
MFN	:	Most-favoured Nations
ND	:	Not Dated
PLO	:	Palestine Liberation Organisation
RBA	:	Royal Bhutan Army
RBP	:	Royal Bhutan Police
RIM	:	Royal Institute of Management
RGOB	:	Royal Government of Bhutan

SAARC	:	South Asian Association for Regional Cooperation
SAPTA	:	SAARC Preferential Trading Arrangement
SAVE	:	SAARC Audio Visual Exchange
SNPA	:	Substantial New Programme of Action
SWAPO	:	South West African People's Organisation
UNDP	:	United Nations Development Programme
UNESCO	:	United Nations Educational, Scientific and Cultural Organisation
UNCDF	:	United Nations Capital Development Fund
UNFPA	:	United Nations Fund for Population Activities
UNIDO	:	United Nations Industrial Development Organisation

1

Bhutan: An Introduction

Bhutan is located between 26°5′and 28°5′ latitude north and 88° and 92° longitude east. It has a north-south distance of 150 km. and an east-west distance of 300 km. It is bounded on the north by Tibet on the west by the Indian state of Sikkim and by the Chumbi Valley of Tibet, and on the east and south by the Indian states of Arunachal Pradesh, Assam and West Bengal.

Bhutan can be divided into three geographical zones: The northern highlands, central zone and southern zone. The northern zone forms the part of the High Himalayas. Its altitude ranges from 3,000 m. to 7,000 m.This zone includes the snow-capped mountain ranges and is characterised by scanty rainfall and the absence of permanent human settlements. It is used mainly for grazing by yak cattle herders. The central zone covers several valleys ranging between 1800 m. to 3500 m. above sea level and has a temperate climate. It comprises the valleys of Ha, Paro, Punakha, Thimphu and Bumthang. The southern zone covers the low foothills and this zone is characterised by heavy rainfall and dense forest. The terrain of Bhutan is most rugged and mountainous and only 7.7 per cent of the land is cultivable and 61.1 per cent is forest.

In Bhutan, there are some mountain ranges which generally run from north to south. Mention may be made of the

Masong-chung Dzong, separating the rivers Amo-chu and the Wang-chu; and the Dokyongla, dividing the Wang-chu and the Mo-chu.[1] The Black Mountain range which also follows a north-south direction, forms the watershed between the Mo-chu and Manas rivers. It divides Bhutan into two parts, ethnographically and linguistically. The Black Mountain range divides eastern from western Bhutan, the Donkyla La range separates Bhutan from Sikkim and the Tawang range separates Bhutan from Arunachal Pradesh.

The main rivers of Bhutan are, from west to east, Amo-chu or Torsa, Raidak or Wang-chu, Sankosh or Mo-chu and Manas. The Torsa, the Raidak and the Sankosh drain western Bhutan, and the Manas and its tributaries drain the eastern part of the country. The rivers of Bhutan are mountain streams. They flow through high rocky terrain. They are not navigable.

Bhutan is a very small country in terms of its size and its population. It has an area of 47,000 sq. km. and its population is about 7,42,737. Its national language is Dzonkha. Thimphu is its capital.

Bhutan is an ancient land of ancient people. According to some scholars, the country is called Bhutan because it is the land of the descedants of the Hindu Sage Kasyapa by his wife Bhuti. The latter's children were called Bhutas and the country of the Bhutas became known as Bhuta-vata or Bhusthan, which later corrupted to Bhutan.[2] Besides, there are several traditional names for Bhutan which indicate its location in southern Himalayas. They are: Lho Jong (The Valleys of the South), Lho Mon Kha Shi (The Southern Mon country of Four Approaches) Lho Jong Men Jong (The Southern Valleys of Medicinal Herbs).[3] Some Bhutanese scholars trace the origin of the name of their country to Bumthang which corrupted to Bhutan.[4] Moreover, the name of Bhutan is generally said to have been derived from the Sanskrit word *Bhotanta* which means the end of the land of Bhot (Tibet).

The history of Bhutan systemically begins with the advent of Buddhism in the eighth century. In 747, Padmasambhava, Buddhist sage, visited Bhutan and introduced Buddhism in the country. Since then Buddhism played an important role in shaping the social, economic, political and cultural evolution of Bhutan. In the centuries that followed, Bhutanese chiefs and monks established their own separate domains in different areas of the country. It was not until the seventeenth century that central authority was established in Bhutan. In 1616, Lama Ngawang Namgyal (1594-1652), a leader of the Drukpa Kargyupa School of Buddhism, united Bhutan and made himself the supreme religious and political head of Bhutan with the title of Shabdrung (before the feet), commonly known as the Dharma Raja. Under his leadership the Drukpa sect of Buddhism became state religion of Bhutan. Hence, the Bhutanese called their country Druk-Yul (the land of Drukpas). Shabdrung Ngawang Namgyal established in Bhutan a unique political system, whereby the temporal and religious authorities were separated and vested in the Druk Desi (temporal Head) and Je Khenpo (spiritual Head) respectively. It was during his reign that Bhutan emerged not only as a distinct political entity but also as a Power to be reckoned with by its neighbours. Tibetans invaded Bhutan in 1639 and again in 1647, but were repulsed. Shabdrung Ngawang Namgyal died in 1651.

Bhutan by and large enjoyed political stability till the end of the seventeenth century but during the second half of the eighteenth century the country witnessed a resurgence of political instability. In the second half of the nineteenth century Bhutan plunged itself into political chaos and instability. There were a number of civil wars during this period as Ponlops (Governors) vied with each other for office and power. In 1907, the monarchy was established in Bhutan to save the country from disintegration. Ugyen Wangchuck, the then Tongsa Ponlop was elected by the Bhutanese chiefs and principal lamas as hereditary king of Bhutan. The establishment of monarchy ushered in an era of peace and stability in Bhutan. Moreover, King Ugyen Wangchuck signed the treaty of 1910 with British India when Bhutan faced threats from China to his kingdom's security.

Since the establishment of monarchy the Bhutanese kings endeavoured to integrate different ethnic groups of their kingdom. There are three main ethnic groups in Bhutan, viz., Sharchops, Ngalops and Lhotshampas. The Sharchops are the indigenous people who reside in north-eastern Bhutan. They belong to the Indo-Mongoloid group and akin to the people of the north-eastern states of India. They speak different dialects and they have their own dress, food habits and festivals. They are about 44 per cent of the population. The Ngalops are the people of Tibetan origin. They migrated to Bhutan between the seventh and the seventeenth century. They are by and large concentrated in western and central Bhutan. They constitute about 28 per cent of the population. The Lhotshampas are the people of Nepalese origin, who reside in southern Bhutan. They migrated to Bhutan since the late nineteenth century. They constitute around 28 per cent of the population.

The second king Jigme Wangchuck (1926-1952) consolidated his authority over the entire kingdom. He also took steps for developing his kingdom by starting a programme of education and training of the Bhutanese students. The third king, Jigme Dorji Wangchuck (1952 -1972) introduced far reaching political, social and economic reforms in the country. He established the Tshogdu (National Assembly), the High Court and the Royal Advisory Council. He initiated the planned development process which helped Bhutan to become an important member of the international community. It was during his regime that Bhutan joined the Colombo Plan in 1962, the Universal Postal Union in 1969 and the United Nation in 1971. Jigme Singye Wangchuck became the fourth king of Bhutan on 22 July 1972 at a young age of 17. Since his coronation in 1974, he dedicated himself to the task of nation-building. He pursued the process of democratisation initiated by king Jigme Dorji Wangchuck and encouraged the Bhutanese people to involve themselves in the country's development. He took a number of initiatives in the foreign policy of his country. He strengthened Bhutan-India cooperation in different fields. He participated in the non-aligned summits since 1976 and SAARC summits since its formation in December 1985. He expanded his kingdom's contacts with the outside world.

Bhutan witnessed a number of significant political developments in years 2005-2008. On 26 March 2005, King Jigme Singye Wangchuck brought about a draft of the Constitution of the Kingdom of Bhutan, which was adopted on 18 July 2008. Under the Constitution, Bhutan has become a democratic constitutional monarchy. It has also been provided in the Constitution that the executive power of the State would be vested in the Lhengye Zhungtshog (Cabinet) headed by the Prime Minister and the country would have a bicameral legislature. The Lower House called the National Assembly has a strength of 47 members to be elected for a term of five years on the basis of universal adult suffrage. The 25-member Upper House is called the National Council. Twenty of its members are elected directly by the people, and five members are nominated by the King. The National Council is a deliberative body and acts on matter affecting the security and sovereignty of the country and the interest of the Bhutanese people. On 14 December 2006, King Jigme Singye Wangchuck announced his abdication and handed over his power as the King and Head of State to his son Jigme Khesar Namgyel Wangchuck. In 2007, two political parties, the People Democratic Party (PDP), the Druk Phuensum Tshogpa (DPT) were formed to participate in Bhutans first general election. The election to the National Assembly was held on 24 March 2008. The Druk Phuensum Tshogpa led by Jigmi Y. Thinley won 44 of the 47 seats in the National Assembly.

The People Democratic Party, headed by Sangay Ngedup, the only other party contesting the polls, won the other three seats. Jigmi Y. Thinley was appointed Prime Minister of Bhutan. It would be as well to study how far the new dispensation in Bhutan continued and changed the foreign policy of the Kingdom. Hence, a study of its foreign policy deserves our attention.

Notes and References

1. Chu means a river; and La, a mountain pass.
2. S. S. Bhattacharya, "Bhutan in the Early Ages," Paper read in the 27th session of the Indian History Congress held at Allahabad on 29th to 31st December 1965, Indian History Congress, Aligarh, 1967, p. 73.
3. See also Kamla Sanskrityayan, Bhutan: The Land and People, Series-16, Delhi, 1971, p. 9.
4. Francoise Pommaret, Bhutan Hong Kong, 1990, pp. 52-53.
5. Karma Dorji, The origin of the name of Bhutan, Letter to Editor, *Kuensel*, 3 August 1996.

2

Foreign Policy: Conceptual Framework

According to George Modelsky, foreign policy is the system of activities evolved by communities for changing the behaviour of other states and for adjusting their own activities to the international environment.[1]

Modelsky points out two types of activities in foreign policy: power input flowing into it and power output it produces.[2] But some states may adopt an isolationalist foreign policy and may refrain from interacting with other states. Modelsky's concept of foreign policy is similar to that of Hans J. Morgenthau who holds that foreign policy objectives must be defined in terms of national interest and must be supported by adequate power.[3] Both Modelsky and Morgenthau imphasise power-input in framing foreign policy. But there are other factors such national culture and tradition and ideals which states take into consideration while formulating their foreign policy. Foreign policy has been defined as "the sum total of principles, interests and objectives which a state formulates in conducting its relations with other states."[4] In fact, the foreign policy of a state is largely determined by its geographical location, size, historical and political traditions, domestic milieu and international setting and economic development.

The Bhutanese people hold that Bhutan is a unique country. They emphasise the uniqueness of their country on the basis of their tradition and culture. Hence, their world-view has largely been influenced by their religion and culture. It would be worthwhile to study all these factors determining Bhutan's foreign policy.

References

1. George Modelsky, A Theory of Foreign Policy, New York,1962, p.6.
2. *Ibid.*, p. 7.
3. Hans J. Morgenthau, Politics Among Nations: The Struggle for Power and Peace, New York, 1963, p.143.
4. A. Appadorai and M. S. Rajan, India's Foreign Policy and Relations, New Delhi, 1985, p. 2.

3

Bhutan's Isolationist Policy: Response to Foreign Aggressions

Bhutan began to face foreign aggressions from two directions, the north and the south, in the eighteenth century. Hence, it adopted an isolationist policy which it considered essential to its survival as an independent political entity. "Isolationism became the fundamental principle of Bhutan's foreign policy."[1]

Aggressions on Bhutan from the north began in the seventeenth century. Tibetans invaded Bhutan several times when Shabdrung Ngawang Namgyal had assumed power in Bhutan, but the Shabdrung repulsed Tibetan invasions.

In the eighteenth century, Tibetan and Chinese interferences into the internal affairs of Bhutan increased inasmuch as Bhutan's domestic situations deteriorated in the wake of Shabdrung Ngawang Namgyal's death. His successors were not strong and capable rulers. As a result, Bhutan faced wars and chaos. In 1728-1729 a civil war took place in the country over the issue of reincarnation of the Shabdrung. Two rival lamas claimed to be the reincarnation of Shabdrung Ngawang Namgyal. The Tibetan ruler intervened in the quarrel between two rival Bhutanese factions led by Desi Mipham Wangpo and Thoudud of Kabi respectively.[2] Moreover, interventions from China took place during the Sino-Nepalese War of 1792, when the Chinese military commander instructed the Bhutanese ruler to support him in the war against Nepal. But the Bhutanese ruler refused to support him. However, China continued to endeavour to establish its political control over Bhutan. In 1793, the decree of the Chinese Emperor which made Tibet a part of China, charged the Amban (Chinese Political Officer) in Tibet with responsibility for the conduct of relations not only with Nepal, but also with Bhutan.[3] In 1884, a civil war took place in Bhutan between two factions. Tshewang Norbu, Ponlop of Paro and Ugyen Wangchuck, Ponlop of Tongsa, revolted against Desi Kawa zangpo, who was supported by Phunshok Dorji and Alu Dorji, Dzongpons of Punakha and Thimphu respectively, for withholding their share of the British subsidy. In the battle of Changlimithang, fought in May 1885, Phuntshok Dorji was killed and Alu Dorji defeated. The latter fled to Tibet and appealed to the Government of Tibet for help against Ponlops of Paro and Tongsa. The Chinese Amban in Lhasa decided to intervene in Bhutanese affairs and summoned a conference at Galing in Sikkim to settle the issue. He made a proposal at the conference that Ha, Lingshi and Gasa, Bhutanese provinces, be transferred to Alu Dorji. As this proposal was designed to divide the Bhutanese territory and destroy its unity, Ugyen Wangchuck refused to implement it.[4] Moreover, when the Anglo-Tibetan war broke out in 1888-89, the Chinese Amban sent a directive to the Government of Bhutan to help Tibet in the war. But Bhutan ignored it and remained neutral in the Anglo-Tibetan war. Nevertheless, China continued to assert its political supremacy over Bhutan. The Manchu emperor, Kuang Hsu (1875-1908) regarded Bhutan as his vassal-state, and conferred upon the Tongsa and Paro Ponlops the titles of Chief and sub-Chief of Bhutan respectively.[5]

In the first decade of the twentieth century China adopted a forward policy towards Tibet and the Himalayan states in the wake of the Younghusband Mission to Lhasa, 1903-04. After 1904, China began to take measures not only to gain control over the Tibetan administration but also bring the Himalayan states of Nepal and Bhutan under its dominance. The Chinese Amban in Lhasa likened the union of China, Tibet, Nepal, Bhutan, and Sikkim to the blending of the five principal colours,viz. yellow, red, blue, black, and green, and emphasised that the amalgamation of these states would produce an excellent political model like a beautiful design resulting from the mingling of colours by a skilful painter. He also compared China to the mouth of a man, and the position of Tibet, Nepal, Bhutan and Sikkim to that of the molar teeth side by side in a man's mouth.[6] Soon after the withdrawal of British troops from the Chumbi valley in 1908, Chinese Amban endeavoured to establish Chinese suzerainty over Bhutan. He wrote a letter to the King of Bhutan stating that his Kingdom was under the suzerainty of China. He also informed the King that he would soon send a Chinese official to Bhutan. In April 1908, Ma Chi Fu, the Popon (Chinese magistrate), accompanied by 20 Chinese soldiers proceeded to Bhutan. However, King Ugyen Wangchuck did not acquiesce in the Chinese pretension to suzerainty over Bhutan. He declined to meet the Chinese official on some pretext and Ma Chi Fu was not able to proceed beyond Paro. However, King Ugyen Wangchuck realised the gravity of Chinese threat to the political independence of his kingdom. He clearly perceived that it was impossible to prevent Manchu expansionism in Bhutan without British protection. Hence, he cast in Bhutan's lot with British India and signed a treaty on 8 January 1910, under which the Government of Bhutan agreed to be guided by the advice of the Government of British India in regard to its external relations. The Government of British India on its part undertook to exercise no interferences in the internal administration of Bhutan. The treaty of 8 January 1910 proved an effective means to checkmate Chinese ambitions in Bhutan. China's aggression had a strong impact on

Bhutan's policy. Bhutan virtually cut off political interactions with its northern neighbours.[7]

Bhutan suffered aggression not only from the north, but also from the south. Its relations with the East India Company began with a war in 1772. The Company was intent on developing trade with Bhutan and through Bhutan with Tibet, but Bhutan was averse to opening its country. The Company took advantage of a conflict between Cooch Behar and Bhutan, and waged a war on the latter on behalf of the former. In the war the British force not only drove the Bhutanese out of Cooch Behar but also captured some Bhutanese territories. However, Warren Hastings, the then Governor of Bengal, made a gesture of goodwill towards Bhutan with a view to promoting trade with the Himalayan states. He returned the Bhutanese territories on the conclusion of war, and sent George Bogle to Bhutan in May 1774. The object of the Bogle mission was to open trade communication with Bhutan and through Bhutan with Tibet. Bogle was instructed to impress on the Deb Raja of Bhutan that the Company had no other aim than that of making it a channel for commerce. Bogle's mission achieved some success. The Company's merchandise could be sent to Bhutan through non-European agents. Bogle, however, could not prevail on the Bhutanese authorities to allow Englishmen to travel into Bhutan. He returned to Bengal in June 1775. Warren Hastings endeavoured to keep up friendly relations with Bhutan but Bhutan-Company relations deteriorated in the wake of Warren Hastings's departure from India.

The annexation of Assam by the Company in 1826 resulted in the extension of Bhutan-Company frontier. Hence, disputes arose frequently between Bhutan and the Company in respect of Assam Dooars. Besides, the issue of extradition of offenders was one of important factors responsible for worsening of the relations. The Company authorities wanted that if any inhabitant of the Company's territories sought refuge in Bhutan after committing crimes in Company's territories, the Government of Bhutan should surrender him to the Company's authorities in India upon request. But the Bhutanese authorities refused to deliver their subjects accused of crimes in the Company's territories and insisted on prosecuting offenders themselves.

The Company authorities alternated the policy of negotiation and the policy of aggression. In 1837, they decided to send an envoy to Bhutan to negotiate with the Government of Bhutan. Captain Pembertain was appointed on 7 August 1837 to proceed on a mission to the Deb Raja of Bhutan, and eventually to the Dalai Lama of Tibet. Pemberton was informed that the object of his mission to Bhutan would be to establish relations between the Government of Bhutan and the Company in India on a sound footing. He was directed to persuade the Government of Bhutan to make over to him the management of the Assam Dooars in lieu of the annual payment of a fixed sum. He was asked to explain to the Bhutanese authorities that the Company had no desire to derive any pecuniary benefit from the transaction and that the proposed cession of the Dooar was to afford the means of improving the relations between the two governments. Besides, Pemberton was instructed to discuss with the Bhutanese authorities the desirability of improving Indo-Bhutanese commercial relations which, though formally agreed upon in the Treaty of 1774, had remained virtually suspended. He was asked to assure the Bhutanese authorities that the Company sought no exclusive advantage from commerce and that its main object was to introduce unrestricted relations between the people of the two countries. However, the Government of Bhutan was unwilling to receive the Company's envoy. When the Company wrote to the Government of Bhutan communicating its intention of sending Pemberton to Bhutan, the latter urged the postponement of the mission. But Pemberton went to Bhutan against the wishes of Bhutanese authorities. He drew up a treaty and submitted it to the Deb Raja on 25 April 1838. The treaty stipulated, among other things, an unrestricted relations between the people of Bhutan and the Company in India; the extradition of offenders, and the right of the police of the Company to enter the Dooars in search of offenders in case the frontier officers of Bhutan failed to arrest the culprits. Pemberton, however, failed to reach an understanding with the Bhutanese authorities. The treaty was not signed by the Deb Raja. Not only did the Bhutanese Government forbid Pemberton to proceed to Tibet, it also refused to forward a letter from him to Lhasa. The Pemberton mission withdrew from Bhutan on 9th May, 1838.[8]

After the failure of the Pemberton mission, the Company authorities shelved the policy of negotiation and embarked on an aggressive policy in dealing with Bhutan. In his report dated 30th November, 1838, Pemberton wrote to the Company that although ill-treatment of his mission would justify the immediate permanent occupation of Bhutanese Dooars, it would be expedient to pursue a less severe policy at that time. He suggested the temporary occupation of the Dooars in Assam. He also emphasised the necessity of the permanent residence of an official of the Company in the Bhutanese capital. In October 1838, the Company occupied two Dooars, Kalling and Booree-goomah. In September 1841, the Company occupied remaining Assam Dooars. The annexation of the Assam Dooars did not improve the relations between the two countries. On the contrary, it aggravated their differences.

In the 1850s the march of events headed towards a confrontation, which was averted by the outbreak of revolt against the Company authorities in India in 1857. After quelling the revolt of 1857, the British Government of India turned its attention to Bhutan. On the failure of the Bhutanese Government to comply with British demands, the British took possession of Ambari Falakata, the Bhutanese territory on the west of Teesta in 1860. But the annexation of Ambari Falakata worsened the relations between Bhutan and the British in India. The Government of British India decided to send a mission to negotiate with the Bhutanese Government. In August 1863, Ashley Eden was appointed to lead a mission to Bhutan. Eden was directed to explain to the Bhutanese Government the reasons for the British withholding the revenue of Ambari Falakata. He was asked to accompany this explanation with a demand for extradition of all captives detained in Bhutan. He was instructed to ask the Bhutanese Government to let the Government of India to appoint an agent in Bhutan. He was also directed to arrange for free commerce between the people of Bhutan and British India. The Bhutanese authorities were disinclined to receive an envoy of British India. Eden went to Bhutan against the wish of the Bhutanese authorities. Eden reached Punakha on 15 March 1864, in spite of all troubles and obstructions on his way. The draft treaty comprising the demands of the British Government of India was submitted to the Government of Bhutan for consideration. After studying the draft treaty, the Bhutanese authorities raised objections to the provisions of the treaty related to the appointment of an agent at Punakha, and to free commerce between the two countries. The Tongsa Penlop stated that a clause should be added to the treaty restoring the Assam Dooars to Bhutan. On 24th March, 1864, when the Bhutanese authorities and Eden sat down to conclude their negotiation, the Tongsa Penlop repeated his demand. When Eden refused to accede to the Bhutanese demand, he was publicly insulted and derided in the Bhutanese court. On 25th March Eden was asked to sign a treaty drawn up by the Bhutanese authorities by which British Government of India was to restore the Assam Dooars, to deliver all Bhutanese slaves and political offenders who had taken refuge in British India, and agree not to encroach on Bhutanese territory. Eden signed the treaty in order just to ensure the safe return of his mission to India. On his return from Bhutan, Eden asked the British Government of India to punish the Bhutanese to avenge the ill-treatment meted out to him at Punakha. The British Government of India completed all preparations for war by the end of November 1864, and commenced hostilities against Bhutan with sophisticated weapons like cannon and artillery. It could have conquered Bhutan. But the British Government of India saw no advantage in the conquest of whole Bhutan. It asked the Government of Bhutan to surrender all Bhutanese Dooars and the hilly territory on the left bank of the Teesta. Moreover, the Government of Bhutan should enter into a treaty of friendship with British Government of India. The Government of Bhutan was not prepared to agree to the terms of treaty laid down by the British Government of India. Consequently, the British brought the Bhutanese authorities round to their terms of peace by threatening to attack Punakha. Bhutan signed the treaty at Sinchula on 11 November 1865, by which it consented to the cession of the Assam and Bengal Dooars and the hilly tract on the left bank of the Teesta.[9]

The war of 1864-65, had a strong impact on Bhutan's foreign policy. It heightened the tendency of the Bhutanese authorities to isolate their country from all contact with the outside world. The Bhutanese authorities feared that if they maintained close relations with the British in India, the latter would interfere in their affairs of their country and ultimately incorporate it into their empire. Hence, they decided to stop all their contact with them. In 1867, they closed the road at Chukha bridge which led to the interior of Bhutan, and no one was allowed to pass either way. They opened the road only when the British Government of India withheld the annual subsidy due to the Bhutanese Government. However, the Bhutanese authorities continued to insulate themselves from the British in India. When the British authorities made some proposals to promote communication between the people of the two countries, the Bhutanese authorities spurned the former's proposals. In 1868, Colonel Haughton, the then Commissioner of Cooch Behar, proposed that the Government of Bhutan should be encouraged to send its young men to British India to get education. The Government of British India sanctioned the proposal for educating a few Bhutanese children at the government school at Darjeeling on a monthly subsistence allowance of Rs 6 each in order to encourage communication between Bhutan and India. However, the Bhutanese authorities showed no interest in the British proposal that the Bhutanese children should be educated in India, but the British authorities persisted in their efforts. Colonel Haughton was instructed to renew his efforts to induce the Government of Bhutan to send its children to Darjeeling for education. The feelings of isolationism were so strong among the Bhutanese authorities that Col. Haughton found it impossible to induce the Bhutanese to send any of their young men to Darjeeling to get education. Hence, he admitted three young Bhutanese who had settled in Sikkim, to school at Darjeeling and allowed them each a subsistence allowance of Rs 6 a month. The British Government of India held that although the young Bhutanese admitted by Col. Haughton to the government school at Darjeeling were natives of Sikkim, their education would be of great advantage to the British Government of India in that it would enable it to keep up communication with the Bhutanese people.

The British Government of India adopted a cautious and conciliatory policy towards Bhutan in the wake of 1864-65 war. It had long been keen to appoint its agent in Bhutan. But it gave up the idea of establishing its agency in the Bhutanese capital in the aftermath of 1864-65 war. It sought instead the appointment of a Bhutanese agent in British India to form a channel of communication with the Government of Bhutan. In September 1868, Col. Haughton suggested to prevail upon the Government of Bhutan to depute an agent to represent it in British India and grant him a "sumptuary allowance." The Government of British India agreed to Haughton's proposal and sanctioned an expenditure of Rs 800 for the residence of the Bhutanese agent in British India and Rs 50 a month as his allowance. Initially the Government of Bhutan did not agree to depute its national to be appointed as agent in British India. Hence, Col. Haughton's interpreter named Fentook was appointed as Bhutanese agent. Although Fentook was not a native of Bhutan, he had visited Bhutan several times and had been the medium of communication between the Bhutanese authorities and the British authorities. Subsequently, Bhutan deputed its own national to be appointed as its agent in British India. Nevertheless, Bhutan continued to isolate itself from the outside world. It was virtually a forbidden land, and no European was allowed to enter it. The Bhutanese authorities refused to grant permission even to European tourists or sportsmen to visit their country. The only visit by a European to Bhutan after the 1864-65 war was the one paid by Captain Anderson in 1897. His object was to collect zoological and botanical specimens. His case was, however, exceptional, for he had been living for three years at Buxa and had succeeded in establishing contact with the Bhutanese authorities and in winning their regard. But he stayed in Bhutan for just about a week and did not go very far from Buxa.[10]

In the wake of 1864-65 war the British Government of India endeavoured to cultivate friendly relations with Bhutan. It sought to convert a resentful Bhutan into a friendly and cooperative neighbour. In 1875, Richard Temple, Lieutenant-Governor of Bengal met the Deb Raja at Buxa and expressed friendship for him. In 1883, when a new Deb Raja was elected, Lieutenant-Governor of Bengal sent him a telescope as a present.

The Bhutanese authorities who had been facing hostile pressures from China reciprocated friendly gestures of the British authorities in India. They endeavoured to mediate between the Government of Tibet and the Government of British India during the Younghusband Mission to Lhasa (1903-04), and provided all manner of assistance to the mission. Ugyen Wangchuck, the then Tongsa Ponlop visited Calcutta at the invitation of the British Government of India on the occasion of the visit of the Prince of Wales in 1905. However, Bhutan continued to follow its isolationist policy. It did not open its country to the outside world. It appointed no representative of foreign government in its country.

Probably Bhutan could have stood up to foreign aggressions, if it had big size and large resources. It could not resist foreign aggressions largely because of its small size. In fact, the size of a state is one of the major determinants of its foreign policy. Hence, it would be quite relevant to study the concept, evolution and foreign policy of small states.

References

1. Leo E. Rose, The Politics of Bhutan, New York, 1977, p. 55.
   Some scholars ascribed Bhutan's isolationist policy to its geographical features. See Nagendra Singh, Bhutan: A Kingdom in the Himalayas, New Delhi, 1972, p. 10.
2. Ram Rahul, "Making of Modern Bhutan" in International Studies, Vol. 19, No. 3, July-September 1980, p. 519.
3. *Ibid.*, p. 522.
4. Bikrama Jit Hasrat, History of Bhutan: Land of the Peaceful Dragon, Thimphu, 1980, p. 121.
5. Rahul, n. 2, p. 524.
6. Kapileshwar Labh, India and Bhutan, New Delhi, 1974, p. 167.
7. *Ibid.* pp.174-75. See also Rahul, n.2, p. 526.
8. *Ibid.* pp. 36-37. See also Political Mission to Bhutan : The Report of R. B. Pemberton, Calcutta, 1865, pp.19-24.
9. *Ibid.*, p. 95.
10. *Ibid.*, pp. 101-02.

4

Foreign Policy of Small States : A Framework of Analysis

The size of a country is one of the major determinants of its foreign policy. By and large, all small states have similar problems with regard to their external environment and their response to them are similar. Hence, it would be apt to study the concept of smallness of states.

The distinction between Great Powers and Small Powers existed through ages. It was, however, during the Napoleonic wars that the distinction was formalised. The Treaty of Chaumont concluded in March 1814, considered those states as small which were not in a position to provide 60,000 men in the event of another French aggression. This definition lays emphasis on military capability of states measured in terms of armed forces. The capability factor is emphasised also by some scholars.

Robert L. Rothstein defines small states as one which recognises that it cannot obtain security primarily by the use of its own capability and it must rely fundamentally on the aid of other states.[1]

The categorisation of states is also considered on the basis of the size of population of states. International organisations like the World Bank, IMF and the Commonwealth have one million population or less as the criterion for defining a small state. According to David Vital, countries with a (a) population up to 10-15 million in the case of economically advanced countries; and (b) population up to 20 million in the case of undeveloped countries could be regarded as small states.[2]

However, the concept of smallness of states was discussed at length at an international seminar on "The Security of Small States", organised by the Bangladesh Institute of International and Strategic Studies, held in Dhaka during 6-8 January 1987. The participants by and large agreed that while quantitative indicators like size, population and resource endowments might provide useful guides, the characteristics of small states also included such non-quantitative factors as different phases of nation-building and development of states. They held that the term, small state, was relative and its applicability might depend on a number of factors. In such a wide perspective, a large number of countries of Asia and Africa were regarded as small states.[3]

The participants deliberated on the problems of insecurities of small states and emphasised the importance of regional cooperation, mutual understanding and confidence among small states for reducing their vulnerabilities and insecurities. They recommended strengthening of the mechanism of the international legal system and the establishment of a UN Commission on identification of potential conflict areas and preventive measures. They also suggested that all possible efforts should be made at various levels to promote international cooperation for peace, security and development.[4]

Emergence of Small States in International Politics

The number and position of small states increased in the aftermath of the First World War. The destruction of Austria-Hungary served as a catalyst for the proliferation of small states.

The First World War was fought on a scale hitherto unknown in history. Europe had been badly battered and had suffered unspeakable horrors and enormous losses. Hence, the League of Nations was established to prevent future wars as well as to regulate international relations. The League of Nations was to consist of a Council consisting of the representatives of the five great Powers and an Assembly representing all states joining the League. The status of small states improved with the establishment of the League of Nations inasmuch as they could become members of the Assembly of the League of Nations. Moreover, the security of small states also seemed to have improved. The Covenant of the League declared that the object of the League was to promote international cooperation and to achieve international peace and security by the acceptance of obligations not to resort to war. Provision was made for the settlement of all disputes between Powers by arbitration and also for economic boycott any Power who would act in disregard of the covenant of the League. However, the hope for peace and security of small states was dashed to the ground with the rise of Fascism and Nazism in the 1930s. The first shock to the League of Nations was given by Japan. In 1931, she violated the League Covenant by occupying the Chinese territory of Manchuria and setting up a puppet state there. China appealed to the League of Nations which condemned this act of aggression. The League of Nations appointed a Commission under Lord Lytton to report. The Commission's report went against Japan. But the fulminations of the League of Nations had no effect on Japan which withdrew from the League of Nations. Moreover, Italy under Mussolini made an unprovoked attack on Abyssinia in 1935. Abyssinia which was a member of the League of Nations appealed to the League against this act of aggression on the part of Italy. The League of Nations declared Italy to be the aggressor and recommended the application of economic sanctions. But the sanctions were applied half-heartedly. Italy withdrew from the League of Nations in 1936. Its action was a shattering blow to the League of Nations. Furthermore, Germany under Hitler violated the Treaty of Versailles and occupied the demilitarised zones of Rhineland in 1935. Hitler annexed Austria and Czechoslovakia in 1938. The Second World War began with the German invasion of Poland in September 1939.

Small states lacked capability to adopt an active foreign policy. According to David Vital, "a small state is more vulnerable to pressure, more likely to give way under stress, more limited in respect of political options open to it and subject to a tighter connection between domestic and external affairs."[5] In the aftermath of the Second World War radical changes took place in the sphere of international politics. The small states by and large adopted active foreign policy. Most of them joined the UN and participated in debates on international issues in the United Nation General Assembly where they flaunted their sovereign equality among states. Moreover, they by and large adopted non-aligned foreign policy. Indeed, "the core of the policy of non-alignment consisted in a country's urge to safeguard its independence, national integrity and national interests and in its freedom to choose its own path in internal development and external policies."[6] However, in the wake of the Second World War the Cold War between the Western and the Soviet blocs was intense. Small states were induced to join either of blocs. But the leaders of non-aligned movement advised small states against aligning with Great Powers. Machiavelli's advice that "a prince ought never to make common cause with one more powerful than himself, unless necessity forces him to it" was rephrased by Gamal Abdel Nasser. He said, "An alliance between a big and a small power is an alliance between the wolf and the sheep and it is bound to end with the wolf devouring the sheep."[7]

The rejection of military alliances by non-aligned countries was largely a response to the Cold War situation. With the relaxation of tension in international politics in the 1970s, non-aligned countries emphasised the need of creation of a new international order based on equitable and non-exploitative inter-state relations. They stressed on the establishment of new international economic order. The third non-aligned summit held in Lusaka was a landmark in this respect. It brought the economic aspect of the non-aligned movement into full focus. The subsequent summits of non-aligned countries in Algiers in 1973, Colombo in 1976, and Havana in 1979, kept up the tempo created in Lusaka.

However, small states remained vulnerable to external interferences and subversion. Bhutan continued to be concerned about its security since the Chinese occupation of Tibet in 1959. When the National Assembly of Bhutan met on 12 May 1968, the King made his inaugural speech highlighting the threats to Bhutan's security in the following words: "Times have changed and the past happy days are over. There is now every danger of the big powers subjugating or destroying small countries (alluding to the Chinese occupation of Tibet). Taking into consideration the present realities of the world situation, we have to work constructively and develop our country. We cannot afford to continue our old ways of life and thought except at a grave risk to our freedom."[8]

In fact, Great Powers especially the US and the Soviet Union continued to intervene in the affairs of small states. In the 1970's and 1980's the US intervened in the affairs of Dominican Republic, Chile, Grenada, and Nicaragua. Similarly, the then Soviet Union intervened in Hungary in 1956, and in Afghanistan in 1979.

In the South Asian region the security of Maldives and Bhutan was endangered towards the end of the 1980s. On 3 November 1988, a coup was organised against the Maldivian Government headed by President Abdul Gayoom by Abdullah Luthfi, a Maldivian businessman with the help of Sri Lankan Tamil mercenaries. When President Gayoom sought help from SAARC countries, the US and Great Britain, India responded speedily by sending military help and the coup was foiled.[9] In the wake of attempted coup in his country, President Gayoom became extremely concerned about its security. In a speech at Male on 26 July 1990, President Gayoom said that some sort of international guarantee for the security of small states was necessary since they could not maintain large army to protect their countries.[10]

In 1989-90, the Bhutanese authorities became very concerned about the security of their country when some ethnic Nepalese rose against the Bhutanese Government and endeavoured to take over the rein of the Government of Bhutan. Some Bhutanese leaders felt that the indigenous people were faced with a real threat to their very survival as a distinct culture and political entity.[11] However, the Bhutanese authorities themselves foiled insurgents' bid to take over power, and staved off external interferences in their country.

Although small states adopted active foreign policy and participated in the meetings of regional and international organisations seeking not only peace and security but also promotion of their political and economic interests, they continued to face the problems of insecurity of their countries in the post-World War period.

References

1. Robert L. Rothstein, Alliance and Small Power, New York, 1968, p. 29.
2. David Vital, The Inequality of States: A Study of Small Power in International Relations, London, 1972.
3. M. Abdul Hafiz and Abdur Rob Khan, ed., Security of Small States, Dhaka, 1987, 1-344.
4. *Ibid.*
5. David Vital, n. 2, p. 3.

6. K. R. Narayanan, "Non-Alignment, Independence, and National Interests" in K. P. Misra and K. R. Narayanan, ed., Non-Alignment in Contemporary International Relations, New Delhi, 1981, p. 95.
7. Cited in Robert L. Rothstein, n.1, p. 117.
8. Cited in B. S. Das, Mission to Bhutan: A Nation in Transition, New Delhi, 1995, p. 39.
9. Shaheen Akhtar, "Determinants of Foreign Policy Behaviour of Small States in South Asia" in Regional Studies, Vol.13, Spring 1995, pp. 83-84.
10. A.G. Noorani, "U.N. and Security of Small States" Indian Express, 6 September 1990.
11. Dasho Jigmi Thinley, Current Situation in Bhutan, in Ramakant and R. C. Misra, ed., Bhutan: Society and Polity, New Delhi, 1996, p. 254.

5

Major Determinants of Bhutan's Foreign Policy in the Post-Second World War Period: External Environment and Domestic Milieu

The post-world war period witnessed the emergence of the Cold War between the then Soviet Union and the United States. The major part of the world was divided into the Western and the Communist blocs. Small states were induced to align with either Western bloc or Communist bloc. The Cold War setting in international politics hardened the isolationist policy of small states. Moreover, Bhutan's external environment seemed hostile to its ruling elite.

Bhutan's Northern Environment: Chinese Occupation of Tibet

In the north the external environment was not congenial for Bhutan. The rise of Communist regime in China was antithetical to the monarchy in Bhutan inasmuch as Red China followed in the footsteps of the Manchu imperialists in its policy towards its southern neighbours. As early as in 1930, Mao Zedong said that the correct boundary of China would include Burma, Bhutan, Nepal, Taiwan, Korea and Ryykyu islands.[1] Soon after establishing itself People's Republic of China sent its People Liberation of Army (PLA) to Tibet. The Chinese action in Tibet had repercussions in its neighbourhood. There was tension in Nepal and Bhutan. It also posed a problem for India as to what policy she should adopt on Tibet. Hence, Prime Minister Jawaharlal Nehru clarified India's policy towards China on Tibet. In a letter to V. K. Krishna Menon, Nehru wrote, "We recognise Chinese suzerainty but at the same time we recognise Tibetan autonomy and the two went together so far as we were concerned."[2]

Till the mid-1950s China simulated to be accommodating and peace-loving towards her southern neighbours. In April 1951, she signed an agreement with Tibet whereby she promised not to alter the existing political system in Tibet or effect any change in the status, functions and powers of the Dalai Lama. She further promised to respect the religious beliefs, customs and habits of the Tibetan people and protect the Tibetan monasteries. In return the Tibetan Government undertook to allow PLA to enter Tibet and consolidate the national defence and to cede to China full control over Tibetan external affairs.[3]

Prime Minister Nehru was taken in by Chinese simulations. In 1954, India and China signed Panchsheel Agreement whereby India recognised Chinese suzerainty over Tibet. Although China and India both emphasised the principle of Panchsheel in foreign relations, there were differences in their perspectives and objectives. While China was intent on promoting her national interest and power, India was keen to promote peace in the region. "For China, the Panchsheel was a diplomatic counterpart of the SEATO, and in her objective she was immensely successful. For India the Panchsheel was an expression of an idealistic approach to international relationship, motivated more by international goodwill than by national interest."[4]

India had believed that China would honour its agreement with Tibet and maintain autonomy of that country, but China was intent on establishing its regime in Tibet. In 1959, the Chinese repression forced the Dalai Lama to leave Tibet for India. The Chinese occupation of Tibet and the assemblage of Chinese troops near Bhutan's northern border alarmed the Bhutanese authorities. Hence they withdrew their representative from Lhasa and sealed off their border with Tibet. The Chinese occupation of Tibet had a strong impact not only on Bhutan but also on India. Dr Rajendra Prasad, the then President of India condemned the betrayal of China on Tibet. He wrote, "We have shown all kinds of friendly feelings ever since the Communist appeared to be coming into power. We trusted them and in the exuberance of our goodwill towards them we accepted and recognised their suzerainty over Tibet. The result has been not only the rape of Tibet but also insidious infiltration into our own country including stealing a big chunk of our territory."[5]

Bhutan's Policy towards China-India Border Dispute

Bhutan followed a cautious policy towards China and staved off Chinese hostility. It remained neutral in Sino-Indian dispute. It did not support the Indian stand that the Mc Mahon line was the valid boundary between India and China.[6] Jigmie Dorji, the then Prime Minister of Bhutan, made it clear that "he would not like his country to involve itself in the Sino-Indian border dispute." When King Jigme Dorji Wangchuck visited India in 1960, he said, "We do not want to be either friends or enemies of China."[7] Moreover, Bhutan maintained a policy of neutrality in the China-India war of 1962.

Bhutan's Policy of Accommodation and Conciliation towards China: Negotiations on Border Disputes

In the aftermath of China-India war of 1962, Bhutan adopted a conciliatory policy towards China and showed friendly gesture by inviting her on the occasion of King Jigme Singye Wangchuck's coronation in 1974.

In fact, China had been spurring Bhutan to enter into direct relations with her for a long time. She took recourse to diverse tactics to realise her objective. On the one hand, she made friendly overtures, as in 1960, she offered considerable economic aid to Bhutan and proposed to initiate direct negotiations on its border dispute, on the other hand, she resorted to coercive tactic by encroaching on Bhutanese territories. Moreover, China attempted to win over the Bhutanese by denigrating and demonising India. In 1964, when Jigmie Dorji, Bhutanese Prime Minister, was assassinated, the Chinese put the blame on India for the assassination. How they endeavoured to alienate the Bhutanese from India may be discerned in what a Jen-min Jihpao commentator wrote about the plotters of the assassination of Jigmie Dorji in 1964. The commentator wrote:

"It is clear to all now that the plotters of assassination were none other than those who have been trying hard to control Bhutan. In the past four years, the tendency for independence and freedom from Indian control was growing in Bhutan. Prime Minister Dorji had made great efforts in this respect. He had rejected India,s aid and hoped that Bhutan would receive aid directly from other countries."[8]

The fact that it was Jigmie Dorji who had favoured closer relations with India rebutted the allegations made by the Chinese. King Jigme Dorji wangchuck explained the actual situation in a statement on 11 December 1964. He said, " the recent event in Bhutan is of a purely internal nature and there is absolutely no foundation in the allegations that the developments have been engineered by the Government of India or any foreign government."[9] The Chinese also propagated against the Bhutan-India treaty of 1949, which provided for Bhutan-India close relationship. In an article published in the People's Daily on 4 April 1984, it was pointed out that "basically Bhutan is a free country, but the 1949 treaty providing for special relationship between India and Bhutan stood in the way of the latter exercising its free and self-determined policy." But the 1949 treaty never stood in the way of Bhutan formulating its independent foreign policy.

The Chinese continued to make incursions into the Bhutanese territory, but in 1979, they intruded deep into western part of Bhutan. The Government of Bhutan considered that it was essential to enter into direct negotiations with China on the delineation and demarcation of its boundary with Tibet. It established informal contacts with China in 1981, and held the first formal talks with China in Beijing on 17 April 1984. Since then several rounds of boundary talks took place between Bhutan and China, but they have not been able to reach final agreement on their boundary. Moreover, Tibetans continued incursions into the Bhutanese territory. They intruded not only into Doklam, Charithang, Sinchulumpa, and Dramana in Western sector, but also in Majathang and Jakarlung in the Central sector of the boundary. In 1995, several members of the National Assembly of Bhutan expressed their concern that if the traditional Bhutanese pasture land were to be occupied by Tibetans, it would adversely affect the economy of the Bhutanese yak herders.They apprehended that since the people living in the northern region mostly depended on the income from their yaks, the loss of the grazing ground would mean the loss of their livelihood.[10]

In 1997, China made a package proposal to Bhutan during the seventh round of boundary talks. She offered to give the Pasmlung and Jakarlung valleys, with an area of 495 sq. km., in the Central sector of the boundary, if Bhutan agreed to concede the areas in the Western sector. China has been motivated by strategic considerations of boundary areas of Western Bhutan. Hence she is disinclined to concede the Bhutanese claim in Western sector and is prepared to exchange the boundary area of Central sector with that of Western sector. But the Bhutanese also insist on their ownership of the pasture land of Western sector, which, they affirm, belonged to them for generations, and was never in dispute in the past.[11]

However, the Bhutanese have been concerned over the boundary dispute with China, lest it should be aggravated. Hence Lyonpo Jigmi Thinley, the then Foreign Minister of Bhutan, signed an interim agreement with his Chinese counterpart during the 12th round of boundary talks in Beijing on 8 December 1998. According to the 1998 agreement, "the two sides agree to maintain peace and tranquility in their border areas, pending a final settlement on the boundary question, and to maintain status quo on the boundary as before March 1959" and "they will also refrain from taking any unilateral action to change the status quo of the boundary." The 19th round of boundary talks which took place in Thimphu on 13 January 2010, resolved to direct the expert group of the two governments to meet and discuss the modalities for a joint field survey. The delegations of the two countries reaffirmed their commitment to resolve the boundary issue at the earliest possible through mutual consultation, understanding and accommodation. They also agreed to maintain peace and tranquility in the Bhutan-China border areas.[12]

Bhutan and China have been in talks for resolving their boundary dispute for more than three decades. Probably any other country with China's size and resources would have been gracious in dealing with a small country like Bhutan. But China has been actuated by strategic considerations and has been intransigent. If China had agreed to the Bhutan-Tibet traditional boundary, Bhutan would have normalised its relations with her.

Bhutan's Southern Environment: India's Friendliness

In contrast to Bhutan's northern environment, its southern neighbourhood was very congenial and friendly in the post-Second World War period. The British were about to withdraw from India and in their place, the Indian National Congress which advocated anti-colonial and anti-imperialist policy and friendship for its neighbours during its freedom struggle was about to come to power under the leadership of Jawaharlal Nehru. Soon after Nehru assumed charge of foreign affairs in the interim Government of India, he laid down the basic framework of India's foreign relations. On 7 September 1946, he said, "We hope to develop close and direct contacts with other nations and to cooperate with them in furtherance of world peace and freedom." He added, "We seek no domination over others and we claim no privileged position over other peoples."[13]

After India became independent on 15 August 1947, India and Bhutan decided to develop a new relationship between the two countries on the basis of friendship and good neighbourlines. They concluded a new treaty on 8 August 1949. Under this treaty India increased Bhutan's annual subsidy to Rs 5 lakhs, while the latter agreed to be guided by the advice of the Government of India in regard to its external affairs. Moreover, India undertook to provide facilities for the carriage by land and water, of Bhutanese produce throughout its territory. The treaty gave Bhutan the right to import with the consent of India such arms and machinery as may be needed for the defence and welfare of Bhutan.[14]

India made a friendly gesture towards Bhutan by agreeing to return 32 sq. miles of territory in the Dewangiri district of Assam. Bhutan coveted this territory for a long time since it was commercially important for the country. In 1919, King Ugyen Wangchuck made a request to the Government of British India to sell Dewangiri to Bhutan, but the latter turned down the request on the ground that tea-garden and plantations would be adversely affected by the advancement of the Bhutanese border.[15] Prime Minister Nehru also faced a strong opposition to his action to transfer the territory to Bhutan. The opposition came not only from the Chief Minister of Assam, but also from some members of Indian Parliament. Nehru bent over backwards to overcome the opposition. He wrote a letter to Gopinath Bardoloi, the then Chief Minister of Assam, on 8 June 1948, explaining the rationale behind the transfer of the territory. He wrote, "About Bhutan's demand for return of certain territory in Assam our position is that we should be as generous as possible without doing any grave injury to our interest in Assam or elsewhere." He added that "if we gave this territory, this would bring them nearer to us in many ways."[16] The matter was raised in Indian Parliament on 7 August 1951. H. V. Kamath stated that the Government of India could not cede or diminish any territory of the Indian Union. In reply Nehru told the members of Parliament to not regard Bhutan as "an alien state." He said, "If we treat them as alien, they cannot come here, we cannot go there. We thought it a very good decision to arrive at to give that area to gain their goodwill. We want the people of Bhutan as a whole to be much closer to India and looking to India not only politically but culturally, than any other place."[17]

Bhutan responded to India's friendly gesture. King Jigme Dorji Wangchuck who ascended the throne of Bhutan in 1952, paid a state visit to India and spent three weeks as a state guest. He participated in the Republic Day celebration of India. The King expressed his happiness at having come to India and established personal contacts with the Indian leaders. He said in reply to Nehru's welcome address that Bhutan's relations had been friendly even in British times, and now they were friendlier. The King thanked Prime Minister Nehru for all the friendliness shown to him. He also invited Nehru to visit Bhutan.[18] In September 1958, Nehru visited Bhutan and in a public meeting at Paro on 24 September, he made it clear to the Bhutanese people that India's only desire for Bhutan was that it should remain independent and choose its own direction and progress.

Prime Minister Nehru said, "Some may think that since India is a great and powerful country and Bhutan is small one, the former might wish to exercise pressure on Bhutan. It is essential that I make it clear to you (Bhutanese people) that our only wish is that you should remain an independent country choosing your own way of life and taking the path of progress according to your will."[19]

The exchange of visits between King Jigme Dorji Wangchuck and Prime Minister Nehru contributed to a better understanding between the two countries. Thus, the foundation of Bhutan-India friendship was established on a firm ground. Sonam T. Rabgaye aptly wrote, "the two visionaries, King Jigme Dorji Wangchuck and Prime Minister Jawaharlal Nehru, are the two architects of India-Bhutan friendship. They not only developed a warm personal rapport, but also laid a strong and durable foundation on which the successive leaders of Bhutan and India have built an enduring edifice of understanding, friendship, trust and cooperation between the two neighbours."[20]

Nehru promised the economic and technical assistance that Bhutan needed for its economic development but the Bhutanese ruling elite were still disinclined to eschew their isolationist policy, and open their country to Indian technical personnel. However, Bhutan's isolationist policy become untenable in the wake of what happened in Tibet in 1959. The Bhutanese authorities realised that the rapid development of their country on modern line was essential for its security and stability. Hence, they threw off their isolationism and became earnest to develop their country with Indian economic and technical assistance. In 1961, they embarked upon a process of planned development of their country with Indian financial and technical aid. One of main reasons why Bhutan could change its foreign policy without any hindrance was that the country enjoyed political stability under the monarchy.

Bhutan's Domestic Milieu

The foreign policy of a country is largely determined by its domestic conditions. Hence, it is appropriate to study Bhutan's domestic milieu.

Bhutan by and large lacked peace and stability in the eighteenth and nineteenth centuries. There were several civil wars in the country. Consequently, Bhutan's relations with its neighbouring countries were usually marked by differences and discords. The establishment of monarchy in 1907, ushered in an era of peace and stability in Bhutan. It manifested itself in the foreign policy of the Kingdom. The Kings of Bhutan successfully avoided conflicts and confrontations with foreign countries.

Until 1989-90, Bhutan by and large remained peaceful. One of reasons for such a domestic milieu was the Bhutanese people had not exposed to modernity prior to 1960. They were virtually cut off from the outside world. Unlike the people of other developing countries, the Bhutanese people had no political and economic aspirations. They had no grievances against their state. Moreover, the Bhutanese Kings emphasised their country's religious and traditional values. They laid stress not only on the material happiness of the Bhutanese people but also on their spiritual happiness. In 1979, King Jigme Singye Wangchuck declared that "Gross National Happiness is more important than Gross National Product." However, Bhutan's peace and stability was endangered in 1989-90, when the ethnic Nepalese especially Nepali immigrants rose against the implementation of the Bhutan Citizenship Act of 1985, and the enforcement of the Driglam Namzha under the leadership of Tek Nath Rizal, former member of the Royal Advisory Council. Tek Nath Rizal accused the Bhutanese Government of violating human rights in Bhutan. He went to Nepal and set up an organisation called the People's Forum for Human Rights in July 1989. Moreover, the Nepali insurgents of Bhutan established a political party called the

Bhutan People's Party (BPP) in June 1990. R. K. Budathoki, President of the BPP, submitted a charter of demands to the King on 26 August 1990. The charter demanded unconditional release of political prisoners, change from absolute monarchy to constitutional monarchy, proportional representation for various ethnic groups in the Bhutanese government, and reform of judiciary. Budathoki asked the Bhutanese King to amend the Bhutan Citizenship Act of 1985. He demanded for the people of Nepalese origin the right to preserve their culture, their style of dress, and their language, besides freedom of religion, press, expression and trade. He also demanded the right to form associations, unions and political parties. Finally, Budathoki asked the King to concede the BPP's demands by 31 August 1990. When the Royal Government of Bhutan refused to concede the BPP's demands, the leaders of the BPP and PFHR organised violent demonstrations against the Bhutanese Government in southern Bhutan. The Bhutanese security forces put down the uprisings. Consequently, a large number of the Nepali Bhutanese began an exodus from southern Bhutan and went to eastern Nepal where they stayed in several refugee camps. The number of Bhutanese refugee increased to around 83,000 by 1993.

The leaders of Nepalese insurgents of Bhutan did not limit themselves to political demands within Bhutan. They started a movement for establishing a "Greater Nepal" by including Darjeeling, Sikkim and Bhutan. In one of the pamphlets distributed by the Nepalese insurgents it was stated:

> It (the Government of Bhutan) would do well to remember that we the Gorkhas of southern Bhutan are not only the majority but we also have 17 million brothers and sisters in Nepal and over 10 million living in India. The borders of the Gorkha state of Sikkim and adjoining districts of Kalimpong and Darjeeling can very easily be extended across the whole of southern Bhutan. Then instead of the Bhutanisation of

southern Bhutan we may see the day when the minority Drukpas of northern Bhutan are themselves Nepalised by the Gorkhas of southern Bhutan.[21]

Many persons held that the threat to the political security of Bhutan and the unity of India posed by the protagonists of "Greater Nepal" was not illusory but real.[22] Moreover, some of the Nepalese insurgents who had left Bhutan resorted to terrorism and indulged in robbing, maiming and kidnapping of those Nepalese who did not agree with them on the situation of Bhutan. King Jigme Singye Wangchuck became concerned over the growing incidence of terrorism in his country. He began to express his concern in international forums. In his address to the Seventh SAARC Summit, held in Dhaka in April 1993, the King said, "Even a small country like Bhutan, which traditionally has been a haven of peace and tranquility, has not been spared the depredations of terrorists who have been trying to subvert our country for the past two years. The spate of violence and destruction unleashed by them has seriously disrupted the process of development and growth in Bhutan. Were it not for the large-scale destruction of schools, health centres, and other social infrastructure by terrorists, in our southern districts, Bhutan would have been in a position to achieve universal primary educational and health coverage long before the year 2000."[23]

Bhutan's domestic crisis resulting from its ethnic conflict had adverse effect on its foreign relations. Traditionally it had friendly relations with Nepal, but serious differences arose between the two countries on the refugee issue. While Nepal wanted to repatriate to Bhutan all those Nepalese Bhutanese who had been living in refugee camps in eastern Nepal, Bhutan was inclined to take back only those Nepalese Bhutanese who had been forcibly evicted from its country. The refugee issue also threatened to involve India. Some Nepalese political elite and intellectuals expected that India should support the movement of Nepalese immigrants in Bhutan and mediate between Nepal and Bhutan in their differences on the refugee issue. Professor Lok Raj Baral considered that India's involvement in the negotiation was imperative for the repatriation of refugees. He held that "by whipping up the bogey of greater Nepal the Bhutanese government succeeded in driving a wedge between the issue of refugee population and India thus desisting India from supporting the Bhutan People's Party (BPP)."[24] But India was not prepared to interfere in Bhutan's internal affairs. She wanted that the issue of Bhutanese refugees living in camps in eastern Nepal should be settled bilaterally between the two countries and any move to internationalise it should be avoided.[25]

References

1. K. P. S. Menon, China: Past and Present, Bombay, 1968, p. 21.
2. S. Gopal, ed., Selected Works of Jawaharlal Nehru, Second Series, Vol. 15, New Delhi, 1993, p. 429.
3. Shanti Prasad Varma, Struggle for the Himalayas: A Study in Sino-Indian Relations, New Delhi, 1971, p. 20.
4. *Ibid.*, p. 271.
5. Gyanvati Darbar, Portrait of a President: Letters of Dr Rajendra Prasad, Vol. 2, New Delhi, 1976.
6. Shanti Prasad Varma, n.3, p.170.
7. Asian Recorder, 28 May-3 June 1961, p. 3802.
8. Survey of China Mainland Press, no. 3221, 19 May1964, pp.13-14.
9. Asian Recorder, 1965, Vol. x1, p. 6227.
10. Kuensel, 21 June 1997.
11. *Ibid.*
12. *Ibid.*, 10-16 July 1999.
13. Jawaharlal Nehru, India's Foreign Policy: Selected Speeches, September 1946—April 1961, Delhi, 1961, p. 2.
14. Foreign Policy of India: Text of Documents, 1947-59, New Delhi, 1959, pp.17-19.
15. Kapileshwar Labh, India and Bhutan, New Delhi, 1974, pp. 209-10.
16. S. Gopal, ed., Selected Works of Jawaharlal Nehru, Second Series, Vol. 6, New Delhi, 1987, p. 324.
17. *Ibid.*, Vol. 16, New Delhi, 1994, pp. 510-11.

18. *Ibid.*, Vol. 24, New Delhi, 1999, pp. 592-93.
19. Foreign Policy of India, n.14, p.15.
20. Sonam T. Rabgye, "Indo-Bhutan Relations" in Ramakant and R. C. Misra, ed., Bhutan: Society and Polity, New Delhi, 1996, p. 286.
21. Cited in B. C. Upreti, "The Nepali Immigrants in Bhutan: Growing Conflict Between National and Ethnic Identities" in Ramakant and R. C. Misra, ed., Bhutan: Society and Polity, New Delhi, 1996, p. 86.
22. Manash Ghosh, The Statesman, 27 July 1991.
23. Text of Address of King Jigme Singye Wangchuck at the Seventh SAARC Summit, Dhaka, April 1993.
24. Lok Raj Baral, "Bhutanese Refugees in Nepal: Insecurity for whom?" in S. D. Muni and Lok Raj Baral, ed., Refugees and Regional Security in South Asia, Delhi, pp.164-66.
25. Hindustan Times, New Delhi, 23 April 1993.

6

Bhutan's Regional Policy: Policy towards India, Nepal, Bangladesh, SAARC and BIMSTEC

After giving up its isolationist policy, Bhutan endeavoured to strengthen its relations with its neighbours.

Policy towards India

King Jigme Dorji Wangchuck had taken steps to promote friendly relations with India. His successors further strengthened Bhutan-India relationship. King Jigme Singye Wangchuck who succeeded his father in 1972, played a very important role in strengthening friendship with India. He paid regular visits to New Delhi and met not only political leaders but interacted with a cross-section of the Indian people. His visits contributed to consolidating friendship with India. During his visit to India in 1985, he said, "Over the years, India and Bhutan have established and strengthened a mutually beneficial relationship. Since the time of Pandit Jawaharlal Nehru and my late father, Jigme Dorji Wangchuck, we have shown to the world that an enlightened and far-sighted leadership can make it possible for a large and powerful country like India to co-exist with a small neighbour like Bhutan in perfect harmony, understanding and friendship."[1]

In July 2006, when King Jigme Singye Wangchuck visited India, he made overtures to the Government of India to update the treaty which was signed between the two countries on 8 August 1949. Since 1949, much water had flowed from the Bhutanese rivers. By the mid-1980s Bhutanese river water was exploited to generate hydroelectricity with the cooperation of India. Towards the end of the twentieth century Bhutan's domestic milieu and external setting underwent a sea change. Bhutan's dependence on India changed into Bhutan-India partnership. Thus, the 1949 treaty became "obsolete" in the changed context of Bhutan-India relations.[2] It needed to be updated with a view to bringing it in conformity with expanded relationship between the two countries. Moreover, there were other reasons for updating the 1949 treaty. Although the 1949 treaty was not an impediment in the way of Bhutan conducting its independent foreign policy, the treaty particularly Art. 2 which provided that "Bhutan agrees to be guided by the advice of the Government of India in regard to its external relations", was described as limiting Bhutan's sovereignty and independence. Hence, Bhutan and India decided to update the 1949 treaty, and they signed the Friendship Treaty in New Delhi on 8 February 2007.

The signing of the Bhutan-India Friendship Treaty opens a new era in the further deepening and strengthening this unique relationship under the reign of the fifth King of Bhutan, Jigme Khesar Namgyel Wangchuck who ascended the Bhutanese throne in 2006. The updated treaty reiterates that there shall be perpetual peace and friendship between Bhutan and India. It removes provisions which have become obsolete over time. It includes new provisions for consolidating and expanding economic cooperation for mutual and long-term benefit, cooperation in the fields of culture, education, health, sports, and science and technology. Articel 2 of the 1949 treaty was removed. Instead, Art. 2 of the 2007 treaty stipulates that Bhutan and India shall cooperate closely with each other on issues relating to their national interests. It also provides that neither government shall allow the use of its territory for activities harmful to the national security and interest of the other. By signing the Friendship Treaty in 2007, Bhutan and India responded to phenomenal changes in their countries, and showed their desire to enhance the relationship to an even higher level of cooperation and goodwill.[3]

Bhutan-India relations bid fair to grow from strength to strength under the reign of King Jigme Khesar Namgyel Wangchuck. Prior to his accession to the throne, the King spent a year as a student at the National Defence College in New Delhi. Speaking at the golden jubilee of the College in October 2010, the King said, "I came to India in early 2005 as a friend of India, appreciative of the role of India in Bhutan's progress. I left a year later as the staunchest proponent of Indo-Bhutan friendship as the key to Bhutan's future, even in this new globalised world."[4] King Jigme Khesar Namgyel Wangchuck visited India in January 2013, and was the Chief Guest at the 64th Republic Day celebrations of India. He thanked the Indian President Pranab Mukherjee for inviting him to attend the Republic Day celebration, but he also offered to people of India his "deepest and most profound affection and goodwill." He said, "My bond with India is for life–for it arises from two loves—my love for India and, my love for Bhutan and my people."[5]

Policy towards Nepal

Bhutan had age-old relations with Nepal. But it was during the reign of the Shabdrung Ngwang Namgyal that Bhutan strengthened its relations with Nepal. Buddhist monks went to Nepal from Bhutan gave spiritual guidance to Nepali rulers. Lam Damchoe Pekar who was later to become the fourth Je Khenpo of Bhutan, served as preceptor in the Nepali court for many years.

The Gorkha Kings in turn offered several estates to the Bhutanese Government which administered these estates directly for many years and constructed several monasteries on them, the most well-known being Phagpa Shinkuen (Swayambhunath) in Kathmandu and Naggarthali in northeastern Nepal. Moreover, Newar artisans and craftsmen of Nepal visited Bhutan during the Shabdrung Ngawang Namgyal's days. Nepali craftsmen decorated beautifully the Togo monastery, north of Thimphu. It was rebuilt and consecrated in 1690, by Tenzin Rabgye (1638-1696), the fourth Debraja of Bhutan. Nepali craftsmen created exquisite images of deities of Mahayana Buddhism, which may still be seen in Bhutanese monasteries.[6] However, Bhutan-Nepal relations became strained in mid 1850s. In Nepal, Buddhist shrines and monasteries were seized by the Nepal Government in the aftermath of the 1854-56 Nepal-Tibet war, because Kathmandu suspected that Bhutan had aided the Tibetans in the war. This had adverse impact on the special relationship between the two countries.[7]

Bhutan endeavoured to cultivate friendly relations with Nepal in the 1960s when it gave up its isolationist policy. In 1969, Prince Namgyal Wangchuck visited Nepal and represented the King of Bhutan at the wedding ceremony of King Birendra Bir Bikram Shah Dev of Nepal. Moreover, the Kings of the two countries met cordially at the Non-aligned and SAARC Summits.

Towards the close of the 1970s Bhutan sought to promote its trade with Nepal. In August 1978, Om Pradhan, then Bhutan's Trade and Industry Secretary, visited Nepal. However, meaningful trade between the two Himalayan kingdoms did not develop because the countries had by and large similar economies.

The formal diplomatic relation between Bhutan and Nepal was established in 1983. The friendship between the two countries started developing and the Bhutan-Nepal Friendship Association was established in November 1989. But Bhutan-Nepal ties received a jolt in the aftermath of the insurgence of Nepali immigrants in 1989-90. Serious differences arose between the two countries over the issue of Bhutanese refugees living in camps in eastern Nepal. The Government of Nepal held that all those who stayed in camps in Nepal (around 100,000) were Bhutanese refugees and should return to Bhutan, but the Government of Bhutan did not accept Nepal's plea that all people living in camps in eastern Nepal are Bhutanese refugees, and refused to take them back. Bhutan and Nepal held 15 rounds of bilateral talks on this issue till 2003. The talks between the two countries were stalled after the Bhutanese members of the Joint Verification Team were attacked and injured in Jhapa on 22 December 2003. Of late, Bhutan and Nepal both evinced their interests in resuming their friendly relations. When Jigmi Y. Thinley and Pushpa Kamal Dahal (Prachanda), Prime Ministers of Bhutan and Nepal respectively met in 2008, on the sidelines of the 63rd session of the UN General Assembly, they agreed to give a fresh look to their relations. They further agreed that the diversification of the relationship of the two countries "should not be held ransom by the single issue of people in the camps."[8]

Policy towards Bangladesh

Bhutan began to take interest in East Pakistan in the beginning of 1971, when political uprisings against Pakistani atrocities became intense. However, King Jigme Dorji Wangchuck had some reservations on India's approach towards the conflict in East Pakistan. But when the King became aware that Bangladesh would be an independent country, he foresaw positive advantages for his kingdom in new political development in the South Asian region. He visualised the possibilities of a regional grouping in which his country could play a significant role. "These factors were at the back of the King's mind when he decided to go all out to support the Indian position."[9] When Bangladesh emerged as an independent country, Bhutan became the second country after India to recognise Bangladesh.

Soon after establishing relations with Bangladesh, Dawa Tsering, Foreign Minister of Bhutan, visited Bangladesh on 15-20 April 1972. Bhutan and Bangladesh both declared their determination to adhere to the policy of non-alignment which played a positive and constructive role in strengthening national sovereignty and independence and the forces of peace and stability in international relations. The two countries expressed their desire to develop trade between their nations. They also thought of developing their water resources through joint ventures.[10]

King Jigme Singye Wangchuck paid a state visit to Bangladesh on 28-30 December 1974. This was the first royal visit of the King of Bhutan to Bangladesh. The visit was an important landmark in strengthening the friendly relations and cooperation between the two countries. The King called on Muhammadullah, the then President of Bangladesh and had friendly and cordial talks with him. Moreover, he held extensive discussions with Prime Minister Sheikh Mujibur Rahman on various matters of mutual interest covering bilateral as well as international issues. The King of Bhutan and the Prime Minister of Bangladesh expressed their determination to further expand their relations.[11]

Bhutan and Bangladesh opened diplomatic missions at ambassadorial level in January 1980. This move paved the way for further cooperation between the two countries. In September 1980, Bhutan and Bangladesh signed an agreement on trade. Under the agreement the two countries agreed to accord to each other the most favoured nation (MFN) treatment in respect of trade. They also undertook to provide means of transportation, warehousing facilities in order to facilitate the movement of goods. In accordance with the agreement, Bhutan could export to Bangladesh dolomite, gypsum, dust coal, slate, graphite, copper and timber products, cardamom, gum, resin, ginger, dry chillies, orange and apple. Bangladesh could export to Bhutan such items as newsprints, jute products, leather and leather products, chemicals and detergents, betel leaves, tea, tobacco, pharmaceutical and medicine.[12]

King Jigme Singye Wangchuck visited Bangladesh in February 1984. During his visit two agreements were signed between Bhutan and Bangladesh. They were the Protocol on Expansion and Regulation of Trade, and Agreement on Economic and Cultural Cooperation.[13] However, trade between Bhutan and Bangladesh had been very slow in growing. In 1986, Bangladesh waived 50 per cent of tariff on imports from Bhutan. The tariff concession gave a boost to Bhutan's export to Bangladesh. Bhutan's exports began to pick up from 1987 onwards. Bhutan which had trade deficit with Bangladesh, began to have a favourable trade balance with the latter. Bhutan's trade surplus rose to about Rs 126.2 million in 1989. Trade with Bangladesh is one of the main sources of hard currency earning for Bhutan, other than the tourism industry. In 2008, the value of trade between the two countries was around Rs 755.96 million, of which orange exports to Bangladesh made up around Rs 160 mn.[14]

Policy towards the South Asian Association for Regional Cooperation (SAARC)

As early as December 1971, when Bangladesh emerged as an independent country, King Jigme Dorji Wangchuck envisaged the formation of regional grouping in South Asia. "He began to see the possibilities of a regional grouping in which Bhutan could play a role not available to it otherwise."[15] However, it was Ziaur Rahman, then President of Bangladesh, who first put forth the idea of regional cooperation in 1977, and began to canvass the idea with other South Asian leaders.[16]

Bhutan welcomed the development of an institutionalised cooperation in South Asia when SAARC was formally launched in 1985. Since then it has been keen to see that the objectives of SAARC are achieved as soon as possible. The main objectives of SAARC are to promote the welfare of the people of South Asia, and to improve the quality of their life; to accelerate economic growth, social progress and cultural development in the region, and to promote and strengthen collective self-reliance among the member countries. Bhutan is of the view that if SAARC experiment were successful, it would improve inter-state relations in South Asia and it would promote the welfare of South Asian people "who are among the poorest and most deprived on this planet."[17]

Bhutan involved itself in SAARC's programmes and activities since its inception. It supported the launching of the SAARC's integrated programme of action, and associated itself in SAARC activities especially in the field of health (fight against leprosy), agriculture (potato cultivation) and postal services.

South Asian regional cooperation assumed a new dimension in Bhutan's foreign policy. Thimphu hosted the third ministerial meeting of South Asian Regional Cooperation on 13 May 1985. In his inaugural address, King Jigme Singye Wangchuck called upon the Heads of South Asian countries to shed inhibitions of the past and look ahead with confidence and courage to shape their future individually and collectively in the best interests of their people and the region. He said that no other region in the world needed harmonious and cooperative relations among its states more than South Asia. The King pointed out that despite historical and cultural bonds existing between the countries of the region, several forces had emerged since the end of the colonial era to sow seeds of dissension, suspicion and hostility in the rank of these states. He stressed that it was essential to the progress of SAARC that all member-countries made every effort to improve relations between and among themselves. He referred to the feelings of nationalism which had given each of South Asian States such a strong sense of nationhood, pride and self-respect that had sometimes created impediments in the development of mutual cooperation among the countries.[18]

The King of Bhutan considered mutual fears and apprehensions between South Asian countries principal obstacles to regional cooperation. Hence he underlined the need for a political understanding to achieve a meaningful breakthrough in the SAARC. At the Dhaka summit, the King said, "It may neither be desirable nor possible to limit discussions in our meetings to issues of non-political nature, for the political climate of our region will undoubtedly cast a long shadow over our deliberations. In the geographical realities of our region it should be unrealistic to ignore the primacy of the political factor, as in the final analysis it will be political environment of the region which will determine the shape and scope of regional cooperation in South Asia." The King added that the main obstacles to regional cooperation were not only the "psychological and emotional barriers of the past but fears, anxieties and apprehensions of the present." He made it clear that if regional cooperation was to be promoted, the Heads of the South Asian States have to "move away from an attitude of suspicion to one of understanding and trust despite major differences in political and security perceptions."[19]

King Jigme Singye Wangchuck wanted to strengthen the popular base of SAARC. Speaking at the second SAARC summit in Bangalore on 16 November 1986, the King called upon the Heads of the South Asian States to inculcate in the minds of the people of the region a sense of regional consciousness and to encourage people-to-people contacts at all levels in order to bring about a greater awareness of each other, and to generate a spirit of friendship and understanding in the region. The King was optimistic that the political milieu of the region could be improved through the instrumentality of the SAARC. He said, "SAARC can and must play a decisive role by fostering better understanding among ourselves and creating an atmosphere conducive to the amicable settlement of differences and the promotion of peace and harmony." Speaking at the Kathmandu summit on 02 November 1987, the King said that the condition of bilateral relations would affect the political environment of the region and determine the future well-being of SAARC. Hence, he suggested to utilise every opportunity for frank and informal exchanges of views on all issues including those of a bilateral nature. He stressed that the Heads of the South Asian States must exercise political will and ensure a political environment in the region which should be conducive to the growth of SAARC.[20]

Bhutan's policy towards the SAARC was influenced by its desire to promote its political and economic interests. Bhutan, like some other countries of South Asia faced the crisis of identity for historical reasons inasmuch as they had no distinct political identities in the past. Pakistan which is one of the two major powers in the region had no separate existence prior to the partition of Indian sub-continent in 1947. Some sections of Pakistani ruling elite held that New Delhi was not reconciled to the partition. The Himalayan kingdoms of Nepal and Bhutan which maintained internal independence during most of their history were under indirect control of the British Indian empire. The ruling elite of Bhutan were especially sensitive on the issue of the international status of their country. On 15 December 1980, when *Bangladesh Times* published an article which made certain remarks about Bhutan's international status, the Royal Bhutanese embassy in Bangladesh refuted the remark in a letter and, wrote, "the Kingdom of Bhutan since 500 AD continues to remain a sovereign and independent nation. It was never a protectorate, and therefore to describe Bhutan as a protectorate and semi-independent is a distortion of historical facts."[21]

Undoubtedly Bhutan is a sovereign and independent country, however, it is wrong to say that "the kingdom of Bhutan since 500 AD continues to remain a sovereign and independent nation." In fact, the term "nation" came in vogue around the seventeenth century. Although the history of Bhutan began with the advent of Buddhism in the country in the seventh century AD, Bhutan emerged as a political entity only in the seventeenth century under the leadership of Shabdrung Ngawang Namgyal (1616-1651). According to Manorma Kohli, Bhutan could not be considered a nation in the Western sense of term till about the close of the decade of the 1960s.[22] As a matter of fact, the ruling elite of the Kingdom of Bhutan were concerned about the international status of their country inasmuch as some scholars held that Bhutan was under the suzerainty of Tibet from 1730 to 1910 when it came under the British protectorate.[23] Hence one of the main goals of Bhutan's foreign policy became to gain international recognition of its status as a sovereign member of the comity of nations without at the same time getting entangled in international politics. Since the 1950s, Bhutan endeavoured to strengthen its sovereignty and independence, and assert its identity in the international community as evident from its decision to issue postage stamps in 1950. Moreover, it became a member of the Colombo Plan in 1962, and joined the Universal Postal Union in 1969, and the United Nations in 1971. Since the 1960s, the Kingdom's socio-economic structure had undergone a change. As a result, the Bhutanese middle class hitherto unknown came into prominence and became vocal about the country's sovereign and independent status. Hence the Government of Bhutan wanted to fulfill the expectations and aspirations of its people by actively participating in the SAARC activities.

Bhutan's policy towards the SAARC was influenced to a great extent by its economic interests. Bhutan, like other South Asian countries, has been a developing country, but it lagged much in developing its economy. Unlike the economy of other countries, the economy of Bhutan remained a barter economy till the end of the 1950s. It lacked adequate economic resources. Thus, it was heavily dependent on external aid for its economic development. Hence it stressed regional cooperation to achieve economic development. Speaking at the Bangalore SAARC Summit on 16 November 1986, King Jigme Singye Wangchuck called upon the member-countries of the SAARC to intensify cooperation and harness the full potential of the region to emerge as a new area of economic growth. He said that the region's rich endowments of water and mineral resources and fertile land were precious assets that could be developed. He emphasised the SAARC's vital role in improving the quality of the South Asian people in the current international economic situation where call for north-south cooperation had yet to produce tangible results. In his speech at the Kathmandu SAARC Summit on 02 November 1987, the King made a strong plea that the Heads of South Asian countries must initiate cooperation in the fields of trade, industry, energy, money and finance in their efforts to achieve self-reliance. He appealed that they must take advantage of the large market provided by the large population of South Asian countries and tap vast reservoir of skilled and unskilled manpower of the region. The King wanted to garner resources for economic development on the regional level. Addressing the SAARC Summit in Colombo on 21 December 1991, the King emphasised the need for mobilising economic resources on the regional level. He regarded the lack of fund as one of the biggest obstacles to the development of economy of South Asian countries, and proposed the establishment of a SAARC Development Fund.[24]

King Jigme Singye Wangchuck underlined a close linkage between peace and development, and expressed concern at the growing threat of a nuclear war. At the Dhaka SAARC Summit the King deplored that the arms race had intensified and assumed new dimensions with the increasing possibility of the development of nuclear weapons in the South Asian region. He made a forceful plea for a meaningful dialogue between the countries concerned to overcome the threat of development of nuclear weapons in South Asia. At the Bangalore SAARC Summit the King called for a concerted efforts to reverse the trends of the increasing possibility of the development of nuclear weapons in the region. At the Kathmandu SAARC Summit he reiterated his concern at the prospect of nuclear weapons development, and pleaded earnestly to take a united stand against that trend. Bhutan desired a nuclear-free world, and supported a general and complete disarmament. It signed Nuclear Non-proliferation Treaty in 1985.

Since 1991, Bhutan faced a serious problem of terrorism. King Jigme Singye Wangchuck endeavoured to tackle the menace of terrorism through the instrumentality of SAARC. Addressing the sixth SAARC Summit in Colombo on 21 December 1991, the King said, "Bhutan, which until recently was a haven of peace and tranquility, is now engaged in a bitter struggle against terrorism. Illegal immigrants and subversive elements in the southern parts of the country have resorted to large scale terrorism to achieve their destructive goals. Many innocent people have been kidnapped and murdered. Large number of basic service facilities like schools and health centres have been destroyed and developmental activities have been seriously affected." Appealing to the Heads of member-countries of the SAARC, the King said, "Our countries have already launched a crusade against this evil through the SAARC Regional Convention on Suppression of Terrorism. We must now work together to eradicate this menace before it engulfs our societies and tears our nations apart."[25] Bhutan stressed the need of dealing with terrorism at the regional level. Speaking at the 17th SAARC Foreign Ministers meeting in New Delhi, on 19 December 1996, Dawa Tsering, the then Foreign Minister of Bhutan, said,

"Terrorism has become a destabilising factor in the region. Even a small country like Bhutan has not been spared the scourge of terrorism. We must all work collectively to eradicate terrorism from our region."[26]

Bhutan expected that the SAARC would bring about tangible improvements in the lives of the people of the South Asian region by the mid-1990s. But the progress made by the SAARC was not to Bhutan's satisfaction. Addressing the eighth SAARC Summit in New Delhi in May 1995, King Jigme Singye Wangchuck emphasised the need for producing concrete results in promoting the welfare of the people and improving their quality of life. He stressed the need for implementing the already identified areas of cooperation instead of expanding the cooperation into new ones. The King said that the SAARC should devote particular attention to areas of cooperation such as agriculture, education, environment and rural development. He also called upon the member- countries of SAARC to put SAARC Preferential Trading Arrangement (SAPTA) into effect.[27]

The Heads of the member-nations of SAARC endorsed the proposal for a SAARC Development Fund (SDF) during the 15th SAARC Summit held in Colombo on 2-3 August 2008. The proposal had been made by King Jigme Singye Wangchuck in 1991. The SAARC Development Fund is mobilised from both within and outside the SAARC region, but its main source is contributions from the member-nations of SAARC. It provides finance to the social, economic and infrastructural development in the region.[28]

The 16th SAARC Summit was held in Thimphu in April 2010. Bhutan hosted the SAARC Summit for the first time. The 16th SAARC Summit issued a joint declaration on climate change to address the adverse effects of climate change in the South Asian region. One of the most significant achievements of this Summit was the decision to develop a "vision statement" by

South Asian Forum. The Forum consists of eminent personalities from diverse backgrounds from the South Asian region. It provides a platform to debate, discuss and exchange ideas on South Asia and its future. Another milestone achievement by the Summit was operationalisation of the South Asian University in New Delhi. The university has become the Centre of excellence for higher learning in South Asia.[29]

Moreover, the hosting of SAARC Summit was a successful stroke of Bhutan foreign policy. It raised its standing in the comity of nations of South Asia.

Bhutan continued to highlight the unfinished agendas of the regional cooperation in the SAARC Summit meetings. At the SAARC Summit held in Kathmandu on 26 November 2014, Bhutan stressed the need to tackle the cross-border crimes like terrorism, trafficking in humans and drugs, as well as to address challenges like climate change and poverty alleviation. It also asked the member-countries of the SAARC to take steps to enhance economic growth in the region through increased intra-regional trade.

Bhutan's Policy towards BIMSTEC

The Bay of Bengal Initiative for Multi-Sectoral Technical and Economic Cooperation (BIMSTEC) is a regional organisation which was set up in 1997. Bhutan became its member in 2004, at the sixth ministerial meeting in Phuket, Thailand. Khandu Wangchuck, then the Foreign Minister of Bhutan, who attended the meeting, said, "It is a step forward in our goal of gradually integrating with the regional and global markets."[30] Bhutan and other member-countries signed an agreement to begin negotiations to establish a free trade area (FTA) by 2017.[31] Besides Bhutan, other members are Bangladesh, India, Myanmar, Sri Lanka, Thailand and Nepal. BIMSTEC is intended to serve as a link between South Asia and South East Asia for better trade, transport and overall development in the region.[32]

The member-countries of BIMSTEC considered that they could utilise culture as an economic activity to help local artisans or artists to create markets for their products. Sangay Ngedup, then the Prime Minister of Bhutan, inaugurated the first BIMSTEC ministerial meeting on Culture on 23 May 2006, and said that it was cultural wealth that has provided Bhutan a framework for a way of life. The meeting explored the possibilities of establishing a cultural industries commission and a cultural industries centre. Jigmi Y. Thinley, then the Prime Minister of Bhutan, participated in the BIMSTEC Summit held in New Delhi on 13 November 2008. He highlighted Bhutan's views on several key regional and international issues affecting his country during the BIMSTEC Summit. He supported the BIMSTEC's initiatives to make the region a free trade zone. He called for promoting greater intra BIMSTEC tourism using the region's rich and diverse culture and history. He also drew attention of BIMSTEC members towards energy problems in the region. He said that the escalating price of energy was a problem that BIMSTEC would have to intensify cooperation and make use of energy resources available in the region.

Jigmi Y. Thinley welcomed the BIMSTEC convention on international terrorism, crime and drug trafficking. He said, "We must conclude this instrument at the earliest and set up practical mechanism for the effective implementation of the convention." He also stressed the need to hasten the work on the programme of poverty alleviation.

Jigmi Y. Thinley emphasised the importance of his country's partnership with the BIMSTEC. He said, "Bhutan stands not only to benefit but can also contribute for the overall development of the region.[33]

References

1. Cited in Sonam T. Rabgye, "Indo-Bhutan Relations" in Ramakant and R. C. Misra, ed., Bhutan: Society and Polity, New Delhi, 1996, pp. 289-90.
2. Manorama Kohli, From Dependency to Interdependence: A Study of Indo-Bhutan Relations, New Delhi, 1993, p. 201.
3. Text of the updated Treaty in Avtar Singh Bhasin, ed., India's Foreign Relations- 2007 Documents, Part-11, New Delhi, 2008, pp.1308-10.
4. Times of India, New Delhi, 29 October 2010.
5. *Ibid.*, 28 January 2013.
6. Dasho Rigzin Dorji, "Zhabdrung Ngawang Namgyal: Father of the Bhutanese nation", Kuensel, 26 February 1994.

   See also Ram Rahul, Royal Bhutan, New Delhi, 1983, p. 55.
7. Leo E. Rose, The Politics of Bhutan, New York, p. 69.
8. Kuensel, 4 October 2008.
9. B. S. Das, Mission to Bhutan: A Nation in Transition, New Delhi, 1995, p. 82.
10. Joint Communique issued at the conclusion of Dawa Tshering's visit to Bangaladesh on 15-20 April 1972, Kuensel, 30 April 1972.
11. Joint Communique issued at the conclusion of the state visit of King Jigme Singye Wangchuck to Bangladesh on 28-30 December 1974, Bangladesh Times, 31 December 1974.
12. Kapileshwar Labh, Bangladesh-Bhutan Partnership in Peace and Economic Development" in S. R. Chakravarty, ed., Foreign Policy of Bangladesh, New Delhi, 1994, pp. 238-39.
13. S. D. Muni, " Bhutan's South Asian Initiatives," Strategic Analysis, Vol. 7, No. 12, March 1984, p. 1002.
14. Kuensel, 16 March 2010.
15. B. S. Das, n. 10, p. 82.
16. Kanti Bajpai, "Bangladesh and SAARC: Origins and Expectations," in S. R. Chakravarty, ed., Foreign Policy of Bangladesh, New Delhi, 1994, p. 244.
17. Achyut Bhandari, "Development of SAARC: A Bhutanese Viewpoint," in SAARC Perspective, Kathmandu, Vol. 2, May 1988, pp. 36-38.
18. Cited in Kapileshwar Labh, "Bhutan and SAARC" in Virendra Narain and B. C. Upreti, ed., SAARC: A Study of Perceptions and Policies, Jaipur, 1991, pp. 123-35.
19. *Ibid.*
20. *Ibid.*
21. Bangladesh Times, 16 December 1980.

22. Manorama Kohli, n. 2, p. 4.
23. Srikant Dutt, "Bhutan's International Position," International Studies, New Delhi, Vol. 20, No. 3-4, July-December 1981, pp. 604-05.
24. Kuensel, 28 December 1991.
25. *Ibid.*
26. *Ibid.*, 28 December 1996.
27. *Ibid.*, 6 May 1995.
28. *Ibid.*, 6 August 2008.
29. *Ibid.*, 30 April 2010.
30. *Ibid.*, 14 February 2004.
31. *Ibid.*, 24 May 2006.
32. *Ibid.*, 15 November 2008.
33. *Ibid.*

7

Bhutan's Global Policy

Since 1971 Bhutan participated not only in the subordinate state system of South Asia but also in the global system. Hence it would be worthwhile to study Bhutan's role in the United Nations, the non-aligned movement and other international organisations.

Formulation of Bhutan's Global Policy in the UN and UN Agencies

On 21 September 1971, Bhutan became a member of the United Nations. Prince Namgyal Wangchuck, leader of the Bhutanese delegation, who addressed the General Assembly on the occasion of the admission of Bhutan to the UN, thanked, on behalf of his King and the people of Bhutan, all members of the UN, and in particular India "which spared no efforts in securing our admission" to the world body. He also said, "this is a historic occasion for us and marks the realisation of one of our most cherished dreams."[1] After Bhutan became a member of the UN, it began to express its views on world affairs.

Bhutan's world-view has largely been shaped by its Buddhist religion and culture. Hence Bhutanese ruling elite have emphasised the importance of peace and principle of peaceful co-existence in their global policy. In his speech in the General Assembly of the UN on 4 October 1972, Dawa Tsering, the then Minister for Foreign Affairs of Bhutan, affirmed his Government's support to the ideals and principles of the UN charter. He said, "We are convinced that the United Nations remains one of the best hopes for mankind's survival."[2] He stated that his country welcomed the prospect of the advent of a new era of real peace in the world resulting from the new relations which were established by President Nixon's visit to China and the then Soviet Union. Bhutan viewed with satisfaction the agreements then signed between the Federal Republic of Germany and Poland, the Four-Power agreement on Berlin and contacts which had then been made between the Federal Republic of Germany and the German Democratic Republic to improve the relations between them. It welcomed the contacts which had then been established between the leaders of South Korea and North Korea to establish durable peace in their countries. It also noted with gratification the visit of Kakuei Tanaka, the then Japanese Prime Minster, to China in September 1972, and the decision which was taken to normalise relations between Japan and China.

Bhutan expressed its desire to ensure that the Indian Ocean and the adjoining areas should be free from becoming an area of confrontation between big powers. It supported the proposal to declare the Indian Ocean as a zone of peace.

Bhutan held that colonialism and racialism constituted a grave threat to international peace and security. It pointed out that such territories as Angola, Mozambique, Southern Rhodesia and Nambia continued to be under foreign colonial occupation. It urged that efforts be made in accelerating the process of liberation of those colonial territories. Bhutan noted with regret that in spite of the pressure of world opinion the Government of South Africa continued to practice policies of apartheid and racial discrimination. It expressed the view that the hands of the UN

Secretary-General should be strengthened so that the UN could act as an effective instrument for ending the evils of colonialism, apartheid and racial discrimination.[3]

Bhutan affirmed that it was totally committed to the concept of general and complete disarmament. It welcomed the agreement signed in Moscow during the visit of President Nixon relating to the joint exploration of the outer space for peaceful purposes. It also supported the proposal to convene a World Disarmament Conference with the participation of all countries of the world. Dago Tshering, the then Permanent Representative of Bhutan to the UN, participated on 8 June 1978, in the 10th special session of the UN General Assembly on disarmament, and stressed the need of general and complete disarmament. He said, "we believe disarmament is a question which concerns the very survival of mankind." He made it clear that "global disarmament—the destruction of all existing lethal weapons and a total ban on the production of new weapons of mass destruction without reservations or exceptions—is the only way to ensure real and lasting peace, security and progress for the people of the world."[4]

Bhutan, like other developing countries, was concerned over the problems of trade and development. It held that great economic inequalities among countries posed a threat to peace in the world. Sangye Penjor, leader of the Bhutanese delegation at the third session of the United Nations Conference on Trade and Development (UNCTAD), Santiago, in Chile, on 24 April 1972, ascribed economic hardship of the developing countries to the low rate of their foreign trade. He said that in spite of several years of sustained efforts to diversify the trade of the developing countries, the pattern, composition and direction of foreign trade of these countries continued to remain basically unaltered. He urged the developed countries to liberalise trade by removing all tariff and non-tariff barriers as also other protectionist measures so that the developing countries could find easy access for their products in the markets of developed countries. The leader of Bhutanese delegation also pleaded that the Conference should pay attention to the economic problems of small land-locked countries.[5]

Bhutan had hoped that the UNCTAD would provide an answer to some of the main causes underlying the gap between the rich and the poor countries of the world. However, Bhutan was disappointed at the outcome of the Third UNCTAD. It hoped, nevertheless, that the UN would be able to provide the necessary impetus and machinery to solve these problems which were of crucial importance to developing countries. Om Pradhan, the then Secretary, Bhutan's Ministry of Trade and Industry, who represented Bhutan at the Fifth UNCTAD in Manila on 16 May 1979, expressed his country's concern over the economic hardship of the least developed among the developing countries. He pointed out that though UNCTAD at its third and fourth sessions had emphasised the urgent need for financial and technical support to the least developed countries, such assistance had seriously lacked. Om Pradhan also deplored the rising protectionist trends and other restrictive trade practices prevalent in the developed countries. He stressed the need of implementing the programme of action for the establishment of the New International Economic Order. He also said that all developing countries would have to be given an increased and fair share in the decision-making process of the management of the world economy.[6]

Dago Tshering, the then Permanent Representative of the Kingdom of Bhutan to the UN, who participated in the plenary session of UN General Assembly on 23 October 1979, highlighted the darkening clouds over the world economic situation. He pointed out that the situation was at its worst in the least developed and landlocked countries owing to the then global economic crises. He held that unless there was a restructuring of the global economic system, the global economic problems could not be resolved.[7]

Moreover, Bhutan raised the issue of economic backwardness of the least developed countries in the meetings of the Group of 77. Om Pradhan, the then Permanent Representative of Bhutan to the UN, who participated in the ministerial meeting of the Group of 77, held in New York on 20 August 1980, highlighted the lack of economic growth in the least developed countries.[8] He pointed out that the least developed countries recorded an average growth rate in GDP per capita of only 0.9 per cent compared to three per cent for developing countries for the 1970-1978 period. Om Pradhan pleaded that the Group of 77 should pay special attention to the case of the least developed countries. Moreover, Rinzin Dorji, the then Joint Director, Bhutan's Ministry of Trade, Industry and Forest, who took part in the ministerial meeting of the Group of 77 in Argentina on 8 April 1983, drew attention of the members of the Group of 77 saying that the implementation of the Substantial New Programme of Action (SNPA), adopted by the UN in 1981, for the least developed countries, was far from satisfactory. Rinzin Dorji urged for substantial flow of assistance to the least developed countries so that they could develop the economy of their countries.[9]

Bhutan highlighted economic problems of the least developed landlocked countries also in the ESCAP meetings. Dawa Tsering participated in the ESCAP meeting on 9 March 1978, and deplored that the development strategy for the second UN development decade had failed to alleviate the growing poverty in the developing countries. He said that the Commission should devise "a sounder and more realistic development strategy" for the following decade. He expressed his hope that in the process of formulating that strategy the Commission would give due consideration to the special problems of the least developed landlocked countries. Dawa Tsering, the then Foreign Minister of Bhutan, in his address to the UN General Assembly on 10 October 1995, identified population growth and environmental degradation as the most serious obstacles to economic development. He also expressed his country's concern over the development of nuclear weapons and threats to world peace resulting from this development. He stressed the need of banning of nuclear tests and eliminating weapons of mass destruction altogether. He said, "the maintenance of global peace and security remains the most pressing challenge for the UN today.

Dawa Tsering further said that the UN needed a degree of reform in order to face the new challenges of the twenty first century. He called for a more equitable distribution of power within the UN, pointing out that Bhutan believed that the Security Council should be expanded to allow greater representation to developing countries. In this context, Dawa Tsering strongly supported India's candidature for a permanent seat on the Security Council. He said, "India's candidature merits serious consideration on the grounds of equitable geographical representation, the large size and enormous potential of Indian economy, and the fact that one-sixth of mankind live in India."[10]

Since 1971, Bhutan formally established diplomatic relations with a number of countries including India (1971), Bangladesh (1973), Nepal (1983), Maldives (1984), Switzerland (1985), Denmark (1985), Sweden (1985), EEC (1985), Netherlands (1985), Norway (1985), Kuwait (1986), Japan (1986), Finland (1986), South Korea (1987), Sri Lanka (1987), Austria (1989), Pakistan (1990), Thailand (1991), Bahrain (1992).

Bhutan, however, steered clear of international power politics and made no efforts to establish formal diplomatic relations either with the United States or with the former Soviet Union. It did not establish diplomatic relations with other permanent members of the UN Security Council because it feared that it would be involved in great power politics. It assailed international power politics. Speaking in the UN General Assembly on 1 October 1979, Dawa Tsering said that the policy of balance of power and sphere of influence only created the competitive arms race between the power blocs, and increased threats to international peace and security. Bhutan emphasised the importance of non-aligned foreign policy.

Formulations of Bhutan's Global Policy in Non-aligned Meetings

Bhutan adopted a non-aligned foreign policy aimed at maintaining friendly relations with all countries. It became a member of the non-aligned movement during the fourth non-aligned summit held in Algiers in 1973. Bhutan made it clear that unlike its pre-1960s isolationist policy, "Our policy of non-alignment is not a negative concept; it is a positive policy in which we judge each issue on its merits."

Sangye Penjor, the then Permanent Representative of Bhutan to the UN and Head of the Bhutanese delegation to the fourth Non-aligned Summit, held in Algiers, participated in the summit conference on 7 September 1973. He said, "Bhutan is committed to the ideals of the UN Charter and its purposes and principles of non-alignment for furthering peace and friendship with all." Penjor made it clear that his government had no intention of plunging itself into the vortex of international politics, but it would not shy away from playing a rightful role in foreign relations on the basis of sovereign equality. He said that his country would follow a policy of peaceful co-existence and would endeavour to reduce tension and increase the area of peace in the region and the world at large. He added that Bhutan would "support whole-heartedly the aims and aspirations of the Non-Alignment Movement and work assiduously for the elimination of all forms of colonialism, racial discrimination and apartheid and join hands with all the members of the Group."[11]

Dawa Tsering, the then Foreign Minister of Bhutan, who represented his country at the Conference of the Foreign Ministers of Non-Aligned countries, Belgrade, in July 1978, emphasised the importance of non-aligned movement for maintaining peace in the world. He said, "The main objective of the Non-Aligned Movement continues to be achievement of peace based on the universal application of the principle of peaceful co-existence, national independence, sovereign equality, non-interference in the internal affairs of states and the right of peoples to self-determination."[12]

Dawa Tsering drew attention to the issues which threatened peace in the world. He referred to the situations prevailing in South Africa, Nambia, Zimbabwe, the Middle East and Cyprus. He condemned the racist policy of South Africa. Dawa Tsering said, "the continuance of the policy of apartheid, oppression, racial discrimination, colonialism and terror in Southern Africa imperils the stability and security of the whole region." He said that his government supported the resolution adopted by the Security Council which had approved mandatory arms embargo against South Africa.

Dawa Tsering expressed concern over aggressive policy of Israel. He strongly condemned colonisation efforts by Israel within its occupied territories. He said, "Israel for her part must stop forthwith to alter the legal status and geographical composition of the territories under occupation." He made it clear that the question of Palestine is at the heart of the problem and without a satisfactory resolution of this problem there will be no lasting peace in the Middle East. Dawa Tseing said, "the inalienable rights of the Palestinian people including the right of their own independent state must be recognised and respected by all." He also expressed concern over the situation in Cyprus. He deplored that a just and lasting solution could not be found yet. He said that Cyprus, a founder member of the Non-Aligned Movement, must be given all possible help by the Movement in its endeavours to safeguard its sovereignty, independence and territorial integrity.

Dawa Tsering highlighted the deteriorating international economic situation. He pointed out that not only the gap between the developed and the developing nations was widening but the gap between the least developed landlocked countries and other developing countries was also widening. He said, "In the present interdependent worlds of ours, world peace and stability are ultimately dependent on resolution of international economic problems." He stressed the need of structural changes in the international economy with a view to establishing a New International Economic Order.

Bhutan emphasised the importance of the principle of non-interference in internal affairs of a country and regarded it as a basic principle of non-alignment. When Democratic Kampuchea was excluded from the ministerial meeting of non-aligned countries held in Havana in September 1979, Bhutan took a strong exception to it. Dawa Tsering who took part in the meeting, said, "We should bear in mind that the present situation in Kampuchea has been created not by a revolution of the people of Kampuchea but by a foreign power in clear violation of the principle of non-interference in internal affairs." He described the action of excluding a sitting member from the conference a dangerous precedent. He urged that the status quo should be maintained on the question of the representation of Democratic Kampuchea.[13]

Bhutan assailed international power politics. It held that the policy of balance of power and spheres of influence which gave rise to competitive arms race between power blocs could only increase the threats to international peace and security. King Jigme Singye Wangchuck who participated in the Non-Aligned Summit meeting in Havana in September 1979, said, "Our deep commitment to non-alignment stems from the philosophy of Lord Buddha. We have based our policy of non-alignment on our determination not to align ourselves with one bloc and hate the other, or to play power politics with both." He held that non-alignment was evolved to safeguard the right of each country to independence and self-determination, to enable each country and people to shape freely their own destiny, and to do this without outside interference, pressures or threats of any kind.

The King expressed his concern over increasing tensions and conflicts in South East Asia. He affirmed that intervention in the internal affairs of states could not be justified under any circumstances whatsoever, as it countered the inalienable right of every state to determine its own social, economic and political system. He maintained that "the principle of non-interference in the internal affairs of states lies at the very heart of non-alignment." He also expressed his anxiety over the situation in the Middle East, which, he said, continued to pose a serious threat to international peace and security. According to him the problem of Palestine remained the crux of situation in the Middle East. He said, "We believe that a just and lasting peace in the region can only be achieved on the basis of total and unconditional withdrawal of Israel from all occupied Arab territories and restoration to the Palestinian people of their national inalienable rights, including the right to return to their homeland and to self-determination."

King Jigme Singye Wangchuck also highlighted the deteriorating international economic situation. He ascribed economic crises to structural imbalances inherent in global economic relations. He said that the problems of protectionism and of international monetary system remained unchanged and the international economy continued to be characterised by rising inflation, unemployment and a marked slide in economic growth. The King said that the economic situation was at its worst in the least developed and landlocked countries. He expressed his hope and confidence that the Summit in Havana would take urgent and special measures to help them.[14]

At the Non-aligned Summit, held in New Delhi in March 1983, King Jigme Singye Wangchuck attempted to explain the concept of non-alignment. He said, "the essence of Non-Alignment is the rejection of all forms of subjugation, dependence, interference and intervention. Its commitment is to the resistance of all pressures— political, economic, military or cultural. Far from being a negative attitude, this is a positive and, indeed, dynamic creed that seeks to promote among nations, the stirring call for Liberty, Equality and Fraternity." He held that the success of the Movement depended on observing four conditions— firstly, the principle of non-interference and non-intervention in the internal and external affairs of states; secondly, the development of international economic co-operation on the basis of equality; thirdly, respect for the independence of non-aligned nations from great powers, and finally, the right to self-determination and independence of all peoples still under colonial rule.

Bhutan welcomed the Manila Declaration on Peaceful Settlement of Disputes, adopted by the thirty-seventh session of the UN General Assembly. The King maintained that the hope expressed in the Declaration was central to the purpose of the non-aligned movement. He said, "we stand committed to peaceful co-existence among nations and to the amicable resolution of all differences.

King Jigme Singye Wangchuck condemned the system of apartheid in South Africa. He expressed concern over the arms build-up in that country and deplored the numerous acts of aggression and intimidation against the frontline states of Angola, Mozambique, Zambia, Zimbabwe, Botswana, Lesotho and Swaziland. He reaffirmed the support of his country for the struggles of the Namibian people under the leadership of SWAPO and expressed his disappointment in the slow advance towards their self-determination. He welcomed the decision of the UN General Assembly to convene an international conference in Paris that year in support of the just cause of the Namibian people. The King also said that he was deeply anguished by the tragic developments that had taken place in West Asia since 1980. He pointed out that "the future of Palestine is the crux of the crisis. It is also the root cause of bitter Arab-Israeli crisis." He made it clear that there could be no just, comprehensive and lasting settlement in West Asia until Israel withdrew totally and unconditionally from all Palestinian and Arab territories occupied since 1967, and until the Palestinian people regained their inalienable rights including the right to self-determination in their homeland. King Jigme Singye Wangchuck also drew attention towards Israel's unprovoked aggression on Lebanon. He affirmed that Bhutan was at one with other members of the non-aligned movement in extending full support to Lebanon's sovereignty, territorial integrity and non-aligned status.

The King emphasised the importance of disarmament. He deplored that several countries continued to spend astronomical amounts on armaments as compared to what was spent on human development. He said that Bhutan both as a member of the non-aligned movement and as a Buddhist state deeply imbued with the values of non-violence and brotherhood, resolutely opposed the insanity of armament and armed struggle. He stressed the need of bringing about general and complete disarmament, particularly nuclear disarmament under effective international control.[15]

By the end of the 1970s, the international politics underwent a change. There was relaxation of tension when the Cold War ebbed in the 1960s. Moreover, the 1970s witnessed a severe crisis in international economy. Hence Bhutan and other non-aligned countries laid emphasis on economic issues at the non-aligned summit meetings.

King Jigme Singye Wangchuck highlighted the problems of international economy at the New Delhi Non-aligned Summit in March 1983. He said, "We are deeply disturbed at the international economy's deteriorating trends. All countries have been affected, but the consequences are most serious for the developing nations of the Third World." The King added that "awesome problems of food, energy, trade and finance will continue to frustrate our aspirations until we are able to restructure the world's economy and establish a New International Economic Order." He drew attention to the huge gap between the developed and developing countries and considered global negotiations essential if the enormous gap could be reduced. The King said, "We must remind our partners in the developed world that the international economy is interdependent, and that prosperity in one continent cannot flourish forever on poverty in another." He urged the New Delhi Summit conference to take steps to ensure that global negotiations were launched at an early date.[16]

The King also attached great importance to economic co-operation among developing countries. He pointed out that the progress in that field had not been satisfactory. He urged the Conference to take measures to make South-South Co-operation meaningful and effective. He said, "the scope of trade and technical co-operation among developing countries are enormous, and such possibilities must be explored and established for all our mutual benefits." He added that those members of non-aligned movement who enjoyed financial advantages and were technologically more advanced, could and must play a leading role. In the Non-aligned Summit held in Harare in September 1986, the King said that it was essential to revive the North-South Dialogue in a spirit of mutual understanding and meaningful cooperation. He also stressed the importance of South-South cooperation and the cooperation among members of the non-aligned movement as a means to enhance their economic potential and strengthen their collective bargaining power in North-South negotiations. Moreover, the King reiterated in the Belgrade Non-aligned Summit held in September 1989, that the Summit conference should enhance its efforts to strengthen South-South cooperation, and increase its efforts to renew the North-South Dialogue with a view to achieving its long standing goal of establishing a New International Economic Order.[17]

References

1. Cited in Kapileshwar Labh, India and Bhutan, New Delhi, 1974, p. 225.
2. Speech made by Dawa Tsering, the then Minister for Foreign Affairs of Royal Government of Bhutan, in the UN General Assembly on 4 October 1972.
3. *Ibid.*
4. Speech made by Dago Tshering, the then Permanent Representative of the Royal Government of Bhutan, at the 10th special session of UN General Assembly devoted to disarmament on 8 June 1978.
5. Speech made by Sangye Penjor, Leader of the Bhutanese delegation at the 3rd UNCTAD, Santiago, Chile, on 24 April 1972.
6. Speech made by Om Pradhan, the then Secretary, Ministry of Trade and Industry, at the 5th UNCTAD, Manila on 16 May 1979.
7. Speech made by Dago Tshering in UN General Assembly on 23 October 1979.
8. Speech made by Om Pradhan at the meeting of the Group of 77, New York on 21 August 1980.
9. Speech made by Rinzin Dorji, the then Joint Director, Bhutan's Ministry of Trade, Industry and Forest, at the meeting of the Group of 77, in Argentina, on 8 April 1983.
10. Speech made by Dawa Tsering in the UN General Assembly on 10 October 1995.
11. Speech made by Sangye Penjor, Permanent Representative to UN and Chief of the Bhutanese delegation at the Fourth Summit of Non-aligned countries on 7 September 1973.
12. Speech made by Dawa Tsering at the Conference of the Foreign Ministers of Non-aligned countries, Belgrade, July 1978.
13. Speech made by Dawa Tsering at the Conference of Foreign Ministers of Non-aligned countries, Havana, September 1979.
14. Speech made by King Jigme Singye Wangchuck at the Summit meeting of Non-aligned countries, Havana, September 1979.

15. Speech made by King Jigme Singye Wangchuck at the Summit meeting of Non-aligned countries, New Delhi, March 1983.
16. Speech made by King Jigme Singye Wangchuck at the Summit meeting of Non-aligned countries, Harare, September 1986.
17. Speech made by King Jigme Singye Wangchuck at the Summit meeting of Non-aligned countries, Belgrade, September 1989.

 (The author obtained the copies of policy statements made in the UN General Assembly and at the Non-aligned meetings from the Royal Government of Bhutan)

8

Bhutan's Foreign Economic Policy

This chapter comprises a study on Bhutan's policy towards foreign aid and trade. Bhutan lagged behind other countries in developing its economy for a long time. It had only subsistence farming and a barter economy till the 1960s. "There was an almost total absence of any basic physical or social infrastructure like roads, health services, communication facilities and schools. Industries were confined to traditional handicrafts. Agriculture and livestock rearing which were carried out in the most traditional methods were the mainstay of the population."[1] In 1961, when King Jigme Dorji Wangchuck embarked on a planned development of his kingdom, Bhutan depended almost entirely on India to finance its First Plan (1961-66) and Second Plan (1966-71). However, King Jigme Singye Wangchuck who succeeded his father in 1972, wanted to achieve economic self-reliance to reduce the dependence of his country on the Indian aid and enhance domestic resources. In his coronation address on 2 June 1974, King Jigme Singye Wangchuck said:

> From year to year, Bhutan is receiving increasing financial and technical assistance from our good friend India. Although the process of socio-economic development was initiated in our country only a few years ago, we have achieved tremendous progress within a short span of time. In spite of this progress, our present internal revenue cannot even meet

> a fraction of our government expenditure. Therefore, the most important task before us at present is to achieve economic self-reliance to ensure the continued progress of our country in the future. Bhutan has a small population, abundant land, and rich natural resources, and sound planning on our part will enable us to realise our aim of economic self-reliance in the near future.[2]

Bhutan's lack of domestic resources and low level of monetisation of its economy stood in the way of realising the goal of its economic self-reliance. Its economic development objectives were not likely to be achieved without foreign aid. Thus, the external aid was essential for Bhutan's developmental efforts.

Bhutan's Aid Policy

Soon after Bhutan became member of the UN and other international organisations, it joined hands with other developing countries in emphasising the need of economic aid especially for landlocked and least developed countries. Hence it started receiving aid from UN agencies like the United Nations Development Programme (UNDP) and the United Nations Capital Development Fund (UNCDF) from its Third Plan (1971-76) onwards. It joined the World Bank and the Asian Development Bank in 1981 and received aid from those institutions for its Fifth Plan (1981-87) and thereafter. Aid received from the UN agencies and international financial institutions was substantial by the Sixth Plan (1987-92).

By 1993, the UN contributed about US$ 275 million covering about every aspect of Bhutan's development efforts. In November 1996, UNCDF committed US$ 800 which was to be spent on developing infrastructure and on development efforts in the district and block levels. In March 1997, the UNDP provided US$ 33 million for Bhutan, which was spent on three areas namely, sustainable livelihood, governance and environment.

Under the sustainable livelihood, UNDP focused on the promotion of the private sector, entrepreneurship, cottage and medium scale industries, and integrated horticulture development. The assistance for governance was used for development management and decentralisation to assist the government in planning, managing and implementing developmental activities. Under environmental assistance the UNDP helped in capacity building and preparation of programme framework.[3]

The UNDP also provided US$ 6.5 million to Bhutan for horticulture development. The assistance was used largely for coordination, marketing, production technology and in developing aromatic and medicinal plants. Bhutan placed a high priority on horticulture development to improve the livelihood of its rural people who comprise about 85 per cent of the population.[4] Besides, the UNDP provided US$ 2.093 million for the management of the Jigme Dorji National Park.[5]

The United Nations Population Fund (UNFPA) provided US$ 4.4 million for country in Bhutan. A major part of the assistance was directed towards reproductive health, supply of contraceptive and communication related to reproductive health. The Royal Government of Bhutan recognised the adverse effect of population growth and drew up a demographic projection in its Eighth Plan (1997-2002).[6]

The multilateral aid to Bhutan rose to US$ 253861776.14 by August 2014. The World Bank Group provided credits and grants to Bhutan through the International Development Association (IDA).

Bilateral Aid to Bhutan

Bhutan received developmental aid from several countries, viz., Australia, Austria, Canada, Denmark, Japan, New Zealand, The Netherland, Norway, Switzerland and India.

Table 1

Multilateral Assistance Received by Bhutan
(In Millions of USD)

Donor	*First Plan 1961-65*	*Second Plan 1966-71*	*Third Plan 1971-76*	*Fourth Plan 1976-81*	*Fifth Plan 1981-87*	*Sixth Plan 1987-92*	*Total*
EEC	-	-	-	-	19.680	-	19.680
UNDP	-	-	2.500	12.250	20.075	21.98	56.743
UN	-	-	-	3.45	11.404	14.354	29.173
UNFPA	-	-	-	-	1.968	1.849	3.817
WFP	-	-	28.500	-	-	16.713	45.213
WHO	-	-	-	-	0.900	3.148	4.048
FAO	-	-	-	-	-	2.000	2.000
UNCDF	-	-	25.470	-	-	10.950	36.420
UNESCO	-	-	-	-	1.436	1.436	1.579
ADB	-	-	-	-	3.723	16.870	20.593
IFAD	-	-	-	0.327	3.350	3.184	6.861
WB	-	-	-	-	2.428	13.756	16.184
Total	-	-	**56.470**	**15.992**	**63.671**	**106.178**	**242.311**

Source: Central Statistical Office of the Planning Commission of Bhutan, Thimpu.

Table 2

IDA: Bhutan

Disbursed Amount (in $)	*Project Name*
15468925.40	Development Policy
7160132.79	Calcium Carbide
5206430.81	Forestry Development
13306354.15	Education
5270691.96	Forestry
33504119.76	Education Development
9557661.15	Development Policy
1422222.41	Inst. Cap. Bldg. Project
1543564.45	Education Development
3330277.95	Technical Assistance
10594185.77	Development Project
11185530.66	Rural Access Roads
825860.47	Forestry Development
4412473.93	Education
5334036.80	HIV/AIDS Prevention
8218068.73	Private Sector Development
12107280.00	Development Policy
6324070.00	Urban Development
7017334.49	Decentralised Rural Development
1082427.76	Wildlife Protection
6025265.56	Rural Communities Development
36841372.00	DPC
10269603.29	Rural Access Project
26172300.00	Development Policy
11681585.85	Development Policy
253861776.14	

Source: www.worldbank.org

Table 3

Bilateral Assistance Received by Bhutan
(In Millions of USD)

Donor	*First Plan 1961-65*	*Second Plan 1965-71*	*Third Plan 1971-76*	*Fourth Plan 1976-21*	*Fifth Plan 1981-87*	*Sixth Plan 1987-92*	*Total*
Australia	-	-	-	0.850	0.504	2.736	4.090
Austria	-	0.047	0.059	0.059	0.142	0.227	0.584
Canada	-	-	-	0.048	0.363	2.207	2.618
Denmark	-	-	-	-	-	25.341	25.341
Germany	-	-	-	-	-	3.707	3.707
Italy	-	-	-	-	0.253	0.385	0.638
Japan	-	-	-	2.310	13.947	39.580	55.837
South Korea	-	-	-	-	-	1.675	1.675
New Zealand	-	-	-	0.005	-	-	0.005
The Netherlands	-	-	-	1.003	1.983	0.051	3.037
Norway	-	-	-	-	2.042	10.518	12.560
Switzerland	-	-	0.489	4.293	13.804	39.307	57.893
Sweden	-	-	-	-	0.174	-	0.174
UK	-	-	-	-	0.636	1.760	2.396
India	4.123	7.777	16.815	32.808	80.900	92.928	235.351
Total	**4.123**	**7.824**	**17.363**	**41.376**	**114.748**	**220.472**	**405.906**

Source: Central Statistical Office of the Planning Commission of Bhutan, Thimpu.

Recent Trends

Bhutan-Australia relationship has been marked by friendship and goodwill. Although the diplomatic relations between Bhutan and Australia were formally established in 2002, a number of Bhutanese students and officials studied in Australian universities since 1960s under the Colombo Plan.[7] Moreover, the Australian assistance covered Bhutan-Australia sheep and wool project, air aviation equipment for Paro airport, and scholarship programmes. In April 2005, the Australian government provided AUD 32,200 grant to the National Woman Association of Bhutan to aid training of rural women for self-employment. It pledged about AUD 4.83 million in development assistance to Bhutan for the 2009-2010 period, a significant rise compared with AUD 1.6 million in the 2004-05 period.[8]

Austrian aid to Bhutan began in 1970, and covered several areas, viz., livestock development, forestry, tourism and hydropower.[9] In 1995, Bhutan set up the Basochhu Hydropower Project in Wangduephodrang with the Austrian assistance amounting to Nu 1,067.5 million. In 2004, the Austrian government committed about Euro 2.5 million to assist Bhutan in establishing a tourism management institute.[10] Moreover, the Rangjung hydropower plant was built in Trashigang with a Nu 200 million grant from Austria.[11]

Canada's aid to Bhutan is significant. Besides Canadian aid, some Canadians dedicated their lives and career to Bhutan primarily in the field of education. Father William Mackey was an educationist of note, who worked as Principal of Sherubtse College in Kanlung, Bhutan in the 1970s. He was followed by Father Gerald E. Leclaire, another Canadian, who took over as Principal of Sherubtse College in the 1970s and remained there till 1989.[12] The Canadian assistance, however, continued. In May 2009, Bhutan-Canada Foundation was formed, and it undertook to recruit Canadian teachers to work in Bhutanese schools.[13]

Denmark has been one of Bhutan's important development partners. It has played a significant role in the socio-economic development of Bhutan. Danish assistance to Bhutan began in the 1980s. Denmark helped develop the Bhutanese media. It provided assistance to the Bhutan Broadcasting Service and the Kuensel Corporation. The Danish assistance was also important in the field of health, environment and urban development. On 19 January 1999, Denmark provided Nu 470 million to assist urban development aimed at improving the water supply and sewerage system and pilot housing schemes in Thimphu and Phuntsholing. In April 2005, the Danish government contributed about Nu 2275 million as assistance to Bhutan's Ninth Five Year Plan (July 2003-June 2008).[14] It provided Nu 1,120 million as assistance for Bhutan's economic development for the 2008-2012 period.[15] Moreover, the DANIDA (Danish International Development Association) assisted Bhutan in upgrading and refashioning its National Assembly into a parliament with modern amenities by funding Nu 22 million.[16]

The cooperation between Bhutan and Germany was initiated by some German individuals who raised about Nu 23 million and built the Punakha hospital in Bhutan in 1996.[17] In 2006, Germany contributed US $ 2.5 million for the promotion of the vocational education and training system in Bhutan.[18] Moreover, Germany has supported several cultural preservation projects in Bhutan. In 2009, Germany provided to 8,000 euros to Bhutan for procuring and distributing rice and maize grinding machines in eight remote mountain villages. It also provided 50,000 euros to the UNICEF for earthquake relief operations in Bhutan.[19]

Bhutan has been one of the biggest beneficiaries of Japan's aid and assistance. The cooperation and friendship between the two countries began in 1964 when Keiji Nishioka, an expert in agriculture, arrived in Bhutan from Japan as a Colombo Plan expert. Keiji Nishioka established the Agricultural Machinery

Centre and launched the National Seed and Plant Protection Programme in Bhutan. He spent over 28 years in Bhutan and modernised farming method in the country.[20]

Japan assisted Bhutan in several fields like agricultural production, human resource development, power generation, telecommunication and the mechanisation of roads. Hundreds of Bhutanese personnel have been trained through the Japan International Cooperation Agency (JICA) in fields like agriculture, communication, and heavy machinery. Moreover, Japan assisted Bhutan in establishing micro hydel power stations in the country. By April 1992, Japan financed building around 13 power stations across Bhutan, which help boost the economic development of the Kingdom.[21] In 1996, it provided 2.378 billion yen (about Nu 725.00 million) to assist Bhutan in the construction of the domestic telecom network in western Bhutan and to increase food production.[22] In 1999, Japan provided a grant of US $ 78.488 million to the Jigme Dorji Wangchuck National Referral Hospital in Thimphu.[23] In August 2005, Japan provided a grant of yen 39.9 million (about Nu 15.5 million) to improve television programmes of the Bhutan Broadcasting Service Corporation.[24]

Japan provided aid for building roads in rural areas of Bhutan. With a grant of 521.90 million yen (US $ 5.73 mn) Bhutan built roads in six eastern districts during 30 July 2006—30 July 2008.[25] On 19 January 2010, Japan provided 597 million yen (US $ 6 mn) for building farm roads in remaining districts of Bhutan. In August 2009, Japan provided equipment worth Nu 300 million grant aid for Bhutan Broadcasting Service Corporation.[26]

Bhutan has cultivated relations with the Netherlands. The diplomatic relation was established between the two countries in June 1985. The "Friends of Bhutan" organisation was founded in the Netherlands in 1988, which donated 35,000 Dutch Guilders for the renovation of irrigation system in the Shemgang region of Bhutan in 1991.[27] In December 1995, the Dutch government contributed US $ 1.3 million to the Bhutan Trust Fund (BTF).[28] In May 2003, it committed Euro 3.5 million (about Nu 194.11 million) yearly for two years, 2004 and 2005, to support projects in the areas of biodiversity, human resource development, and to preserve and promote culture of Bhutan.[29] In 2008, the Netherlands provided aid of Euro 10 million to Bhutan for its 10th five-year plan.[30]

Bhutan has established friendly relations with Norway. In 1997, the Government of Norway provided 21 million Norwegian kroners (about Nu 95 million) for a feasibility study of the 265 MW Mangdue Chhu Hydroelectric Project.[31] Norway also provided 13.9 million kroners (about US $ 2 million) to the Bhutan Trust Fund (BTF) for environmental programme.[32]

Norway is one of the biggest donors to the BTF. In December 2009, it contributed Norwegian kroner 1800,000 (US $300,000) to the BTF. This contribution by Norway is in addition to its earlier contribution of US $ 988,371, thus contributing a total of US $ 1,2888 million to the fund.[33]

The cooperation between Bhutan and Switzerland began in the 1950s through friendship between King Jigme Dorji Wangchuck and a rich Swiss businessman, Fritz Von Schulthess. Later some other rich Swiss nationals offered aid for development activities in Bhutan, and a "foundation pro Bhutan" was established. In 1975, Helvetas (Swiss Association for International Cooperation) took over the activities of the foundation. In February 1995, Helvetas contributed Nu 38 million in assistance to the Natural Resources Training Institute, helped to establish. By 1995, Bhutanese-Swiss cooperation grew into one of the largest bilateral cooperation The Swiss aid agency, Helvetas, which involved itself in Bhutan's development, celebrated '20 years in Bhutan' in July 1995.[34] Switzerland has been an important partner in socio-economic development of Bhutan. It contributed around Nu 1,200 million to the educational system of Bhutan. It financed the renovations of the buildings of the colleges of education in Paro and Samse from the mid-1980s to February 2010.[35] Moreover, Switzerland and the European Union have undertaken a project to preserve and leverage Bhutan's unique cultural diversity. They have committed Nu 39 million for the project.[36] Switzerland also provided assistance to Bhutan in the field of healthcare as early as 1974, when a hospital was established in Wangdicholing which was developed into 40-bed hospital in 1992.[37]

Bhutan and Thailand both follow Buddhism and the two countries are under monarchical rule. Bhutan has cultivated friendly relations with Thailand. In 1998, it organised a week-long Bhutan Festival in Bangkok from 12 to 18 October, featuring dancers and musicians from Thimphu's Royal Academy of Performing Arts, an exhibition of thangkas, handicrafts, jewellery, textiles, books and photographs, a fashion show titled, "Bhutan: Paradise of the Himalayas", and a food festival prepared by chefs from Thimphu.[38] The cooperation between Bhutan and Thailand started in the health sector and human resource development. Several Bhutanese doctors, nurses and technicians have been trained in Thailand. Thai health personnel also have been visiting Bhutan to provide health services.[39]

India has been Bhutan's largest development partner. Since 1961, when the Royal Government of Bhutan embarked on its First Five Year Plan, Bhutan completed ten Five Year Plans. Some of the major development projects implemented in Bhutan with Indian assistance are Paro airport, Bhutan Broadcasting Station, a network of roads, microwave links, geological and mineral surveys, the Chukha (336 MW), Kurichhu (60 MW) and Tala (1020 MW), the Penden Cement Plant, the Dungsam Cement Plant, several schools and hospitals. India's assistance to Bhutan's 10th Five Year Plan (July 2008—June 2013) was Nu 34 billion of the total Nu 74 billion capital expenditure.[40] Moreover, India has been assisting Bhutan in completing its hydropower projects.

Bhutan and India signed an agreement on 28 July 2007, to build the Punatsangchhu-1 Hydropower Project (1095 MW). The estimated cost of the project is Nu 38,148.10 million. The project would be funded by India with 40 per cent grant and 60 per cent loan. Bhutan and India have agreed to build Hydropower Projects of 10,000 MW by 2020. They also agreed to start the Punatsangchhu-11(1000 MW), Mangdechhu (720 MW) and Sankosh (4060 MW) hydropower projects at the estimated cost of Nu 500 billion. Apart from ongoing Punatsangchhu-1, all other projects to produce 10,000 MW by 2020 would be built on a 70 per cent loan and 30 per cent grant basis.[41] Bhutan has agreed to sell all surplus power to India. Thus, India would benefit from the implementation of these hydropower projects.

Bhutan leveraged foreign assistance to boost its economic development. It also augmented its economic resources through its foreign trade.

Bhutan's Foreign Trade

Prior to the period of its planned economic development, Bhutan had very little foreign trade. By and large the Bhutanese traders were engaged in barter trade. They served as intermediaries for the exchange of several commodities between Tibet and India. They brought musk, horses, dried chillies, walnuts, yak tails, woollen goods, gold, and silver from Tibet and exchanged them for Indian goods like indigo, clove, tobacco, betel leaves, cotton cloth and dried fish. Bhutan's trade with Tibet was banned in 1960, sequel to China's suppression of Tibet's autonomy. Since then India has been its main trade partner.

Towards the end of the 1970s Bhutan sought to diversify its foreign trade. In August 1978, it sent a trade delegation to Nepal with a view to establishing trade relations with that country.

Table 4

Bhutan's Overall Balance of Trade
(In Ngultrums)

Year	*Country*	*Imports*	*Exports*	*Balance*
1981	Bangladesh	1,210	-	-1,210
	India	451,024,000	164,440,000	-286,584,000
	Others	65,309,892	9,717,498	-55,592,394
TOTAL		**516,335,102**	**174,157,498**	**-342,177,604**
1982	Bangladesh	3,850	-	-3,850
	India	440,227,318	155,206,252	-285,021,066
	Others	100,015,676	7,016,009	-92,999,667
TOTAL		**540,246,844**	**162,222,261**	**-378,024,583**
1983	Bangladesh	35,696	-	-35,696
	India	409,002,510	158,212,795	-250,789,715
	Others	129,335,149	6,633,332	-122,701,817
TOTAL		**538,373**	**164,846,127**	**-373,527,228**
1984	Bangladesh	134,961	8,504	-126,457
	India	673,626,000	193,190,099	-480,435,901
	Others	99,875,751	10,837,200	-89,038,551
TOTAL		**773,636,712**	**204,035,803**	**-569,600,909**

(Contd...)

Year	*Country*	*Imports*	*Exports*	*Balance*
1985	Bangladesh	943,769	248,900	-694,869
	India	829,418,258	265,187,327	-564,230,931
	Others	92,493,435	6,113,607	-86,379,828
TOTAL		**922,855,462**	**271,549,834**	**-651,305,628**
1986	Bangladesh	-	-	-
	India	829,507,636	373,664,093	-455,843,543
	Others	354,003,068	7,256,550	-346,746,518
TOTAL		**1,183,510,704**	**380,920,643**	**-802,590,061**
1987	Bangladesh	168,159	402,876	−234,717
	India	985,177,145	695,715,137	-199,462,008
	Others	225,046,003	12,175,816	-212,870,187
TOTAL		**1,120,391,307**	**708,293,829**	**-412,097,478**
1988	Bangladesh	1,483,037	28,767,278	+27,284,241
	India	1,108,895,447	989,250,553	-119,644,894
	Others	662,309,375	23,475,199	-638,834,176
TOTAL		**1,772,687,859**	**1,041,493,030**	**-731,194,829**
1989	Bangladesh	1,467,441	127,745,419	+126,277,978
	India	1,214,811,637	985,927,144	-228,884,493
	Others	248,411,926	18,652,658	-229,759,268
TOTAL		**1,464,691,004**	**1,132,325,221**	**-332,365,783**

Source: Royal Government of Bhutan, Department of Revenue and Customs, Thimpu.

However, meaningful trade between the two Himalayan kingdoms did not develop because the two countries had almost similar economies. In September 1980, Bhutan signed a trade agreement with Bangladesh. The two countries agreed to accord the most-favoured nation (MFN) treatment to each other in the matter of trade. However, trade between Bhutan and Bangladesh was very slow to pick up. In 1986, Bangladesh waived 50 per cent of the tariff on imports from Bhutan. The tariff concession by Bangladesh boosted Bhutan's exports. In the years 1987-89, Bhutan had a favourable balance of trade with Bangladesh. Moreover, Bhutan succeeded in establishing trade relations with other third countries towards the end of the 1980s. Table 4 indicates expansion and diversification of Bhutan's foreign trade.

India continued to be Bhutan's most important trade partner. Bhutan's exports to India have increased more than five times since 1981. The increase became dramatic in 1987 owing largely to the export of electricity from the Chukha Project. However, Bhutan's trade deficit continued to increase. In years 2004-05, Bhutan's trade deficit grew to about Nu 10 billion following the surge in imports brought about by the purchase of two Airbus aircrafts by Druk Air.[42] Of the total imports in 2005, 75.1 per cent were from India. Import from Germany accounted for 22.8 per cent on account of the purchase of two Airbus aircraft followed by Japan at 3.8 per cent, Singapore, Thailand and South Korea. Main items of imports from India were mineral, oils and fuel, base metal and base products, machinery and mechanical appliances and prepared food stuff. Machinery, electronics, textiles, medicines and pharmaceutical, food products, plastic and rubber goods were the imports from countries other than India in 2005.[43]

India continued to be Bhutan's main destination for exports accounting for 87.6 per cent of Bhutan's total exports in 2005.

Hong Kong was at second place with six per cent of total exports pushing Bangladesh to third place with 4.9 per cent. Hydropower continued to be Bhutan's main export to India accounting for 25.7 per cent of merchandise exports, earning Nu 3.4 billion in 2005. Bhutan's increasing trade deficit is likely to be neutralised by growing export of electricity with the completion of its hydropower projects.

References

1. Yeshey Zimba, "Bhutan: Three Decades of Planned Development" in Ramakant and R. C. Misra, ed., Bhutan: Society and Polity, New Delhi, 1996, p. 169.
2. Bhutan: Development in Himalayan Kingdom, World Bank Report 4307-BHU. 7 April 1983. p. 99.
3. Kuensel, 22 March 1997.
4. Kuensel, 19 July 1997.
5. Kuensel, 30 August 1997.
6. *Ibid.*
7. Kuensel, 10 October 1998.
8. Kuensel, 10 February 2010.
9. Kuensel, 7 January 1995.
10. Kuensel, 15 April 1995.
11. Kuensel, 24 August 2005.
12. Kuensel, 21 April 2010.
13. Kuensel, 29 May 2010.
14. Kuensel, 6 April 2005.
15. Kuensel, 28 March 2007.
16. Kuensel, 5 January 2008.
17. Kuensel, 5 October 1996.
18. Kuensel, 18 March 2006.
19. Kuensel, 5 December 2009.
20. Kuensel, 28 March 1992.
21. Kuensel, 2 May 1992.
22. Kuensel, 9 October 1993.
23. Kuensel, 11 December 1999.
24. Kuensel, 10 August 2005.
25. Kuensel, 18 August 2009.

26. Kuensel, 20 January 2010.
27. Kuensel, 23 November 1991.
28. Kuensel, 30 December 1995.
29. Kuensel, 24 May 2003.
30. Kuensel, 30 July 2008.
31. Kuensel, 23 August 1997.
32. Kuensel, 13 September 1997.

    The Bhutan Trust Fund became operational in 1991 with contributions from the Global Environment Facility, WWF-US, the governments of the Netherlands, Norway, Denmark and Switzerland. *Ibid.*
33. Kuensel, 03 December 2009.
34. Kuensel, 15 July 1995.
35. Kuensel, 11 February 2010.
36. Kuensel, 09 April 2010.
37. Kuensel, 10 June 2010.
38. Kuensel, 14 November 1998.
39. Kuensel, 19 June 2004.
40. Kuensel, o4 February 2010.
41. Kuensel, 11 February 2010.
42. Kuensel, 21 March 2007.
43. *Ibid.*

9

Bhutan, China and India

Bhutan has been taking steps to strengthen its friendships with India, but its relations with China remain more or less frozen. It has not established its diplomatic relations with China, let alone economic and cultural relations. This chapter comprises a study of the factors which have stood in the way of normalisation of its ties with China. It also includes a study of the factors which help grow friendly relations with India.

Bhutan's Stand-offish Relations Towards China : Response to Tibetan and Chinese Hostilities

The main factor behind the absence of thaw in Bhutan's relationship with its northern neighbours has been the latter's hostile attitudes towards the former since its inception. In the seventeenth century when Bhutan emerged as a united and strong country under Lama Ngawang Namgyal, Tibetans invaded Bhutan several times but they were repulsed by the Bhutanese ruler. While Lama Ngawang Namgyal was at the helm of Bhutanese affairs, Tibetans were not able to interfere in the internal affairs of Bhutan, but Lama Ngawang Namgyal died in 1651.

After the death of Lama Ngawang Namgyal, Bhutan's political condition deteriorated. His successors were not able rulers and they could not maintain political peace and unity in the country. Dissensions and differences emerged among Bhutanese chiefs. Hence Bhutan became weak. Hence Tibet again invaded Bhutan in 1676. However, King Deldan Namgyal of Ladakh took up the cause of Bhutan and sided with the Bhutanese in the Tibet-Bhutan war as the people of Ladakh belonged to the same school of Lamaism as the people of Bhutan, viz., the Drukpa Kagypa. Tibet was so incensed at Ladakh for siding with Bhutan that it invaded Ladakh in 1679. King Delden Namgyal of Ladakh was unable to repulse the Mongol-Tibetan invaders. Eventually the Mughal ruler of India intervened on behalf of Ladakh and the Mughal forces compelled the Mongol-Tibetan army to withdraw from the frontier of Ladakh. However, Lhazang Khan, the Khoshot Mongol ruler of Tibet again attacked Bhutan in 1714.[1]

The Tibetans again intervened in Bhutanese affairs in 1728-29, when two rival lamas of Bhutan started fighting over the issue of the reincarnation of Shabdrung Ngawang Namgyal. The two rival Bhutanese factions were led by Desi Mipham Wangpo and Thondub of Kabi respectively. Towards the end of 1730, the Tibetan ruler intervened in the dispute between the two rival Bhutanese lamas and brought about a settlement of the dispute in 1731. According to terms of settlement, Bhutan agreed to pay respects and offer presents to the ruler of Tibet. Thus, the ruler of Tibet succeeded in establishing his influence over Bhutan by a clever exploitation of dissensions in Bhutan. The Tibetan interference in Bhutanese affairs in 1730-31, and the conclusion of settlement of their discord through Tibetan mediation led some scholars to hold that Bhutan remained under the suzerainty of Tibet from 1730 to 1910. However, the Bhutanese people maintain that their country has never been under any foreign rule and has been independent since its inception.[2]

Towards the mid-eighteenth century China strengthened its military power and adopted expansionist policy. It established its suzerainty over Tibet and appointed its Amban (Political Officer) in Lhasa. It started extending its power over Bhutan through its control over Tibet. During the Sino-Nepalese war of 1789-92, China endeavoured to assert its power over the Himalayan Kingdom. Its military general, Fu Kang-an, asked the Bhutanese to support the Chinese in the war. In the war Nepal suffered a series of defeats and concluded a humiliating agreement with China on 30 September 1792. According to the terms of the agreement, Nepal undertook to submit its disputes with Tibet to the Amban in Lhasa for settlement; it agreed to send a mission to Peking every five years with gifts for the Chinese emperor. In the wake of the Sino-Nepalese war of 1789-92, China attempted to extend its political influence over the Himalayan states, and started defining its relationship with the Himalayan countries of Nepal, Bhutan and Sikkim in terms of its vassal states. In 1793, the Chinese emperor issued a decree which made Tibet a part of China and charged the Amban in Lhasa with exclusive responsibility for the conduct of Tibet's relations not only with Nepal but also with Bhutan and Sikkim.[3]

The Tibetans and Chinese attempted to interfere in Bhutan's internal affairs in 1884-85, when a civil war took place between rival factions of Bhutan, one faction was led Tshewang Norbu, Ponlop of Paro, Ugyen Wangchuk, Ponlop of Tongsa, and another faction was led by Desi Kawa Zangpo, Phuntshok Dorji and Alu Dorji, Dzongpons of Punakha and Thimphu respectively. They fought a battle in May 1885 over the issue of their share of the British subsidy. Phunshok Dorji was killed in the battle and Alu Dorji fled to Tibet and appealed to the Tibetan government for help against Ponlops of Paro and Tongsa. The Chinese Amban in Lhasa decided to intervene in Bhutanese affairs and summoned a conference at Galing in Sikkim to settle the issue. He made a proposal at the conference that a few provinces of Bhutan be given to Alu Dorji. As this proposal was designed to divide the Kingdom of Bhutan, King Ugyen Wangchuck refused to implement it. The Chinese Amban again attempted to assert his political power over Bhutan and sent a directive to the Bhutanese government to help Tibet in the Anglo-Tibetan war in 1888-89.[4] As a matter of fact, China considered Bhutan as its vassal-state.

Towards the close of the first decade of the twentieth century China resolved to give effect to its claim to suzerainty over Bhutan. The presence of British troops in the Chumbi Valley was a powerful deterrent to China's expansionist policy. The withdrawal of those troops in January 1908, provided a fillip to China's ambitions. Soon after the withdrawal of British troops, the Chinese Amban in Lhasa endeavoured to establish Chinese suzerainty over Bhutan. He wrote to the King of Bhutan stating that Bhutan was the southern gate of the Chinese empire. He asserted that Bhutan lay under the suzerainty of China and informed the Bhutanese King that he would soon send a Chinese official to Bhutan. In April 1908, Ma Chi Fu, the Chinese Popon (the Chinese magistrate) accompanied by twenty Chinese soldiers proceeded to Bhutan. However, King Ugyen Wangchuck did not acquiesce in the Chinese claim of suzerainty over his kingdom. He declined to meet Ma Chi Fu who was not able to proceed beyond Paro.[5] However, it is apt to examine China's claim to suzerainty over Bhutan in view of the former's assertion on the issue.

An Appraisal of China's Claim to Suzerainty over Bhutan

A state under suzerainty is considered a mere part of the state which enjoys suzerainty over it and is mainly represented internationally by the suzerain state. All international treaties concluded by the suzerain state are binding upon vassal state, if a clause making the latter an exception to this rule is not specifically included. If the suzerain state embarks upon a war, the vassal state is also *ipso facto* at war on the side of the suzerain state. Besides, the suzerain state is responsible to some extent for all actions of the vassal state.[6]

The modern history of Bhutan makes it obvious that the ruling elites of Bhutan were masters of their own affairs and that no foreign Power had ever exercised any control over them. Bhutan never joined the Chinese or Tibetans in a war against a foreign Power. China fought with Britain in 1838-42 and 1859-61, and with Japan in 1894. Tibet fought wars with Nepal in 1789-92 and in 1854-56, and with the British in 1888, but in all these wars, Bhutan was neutral. Moreover, Bhutan conducted its foreign relations independently of China or Tibet. As early as the beginning of the eighteenth century, Bhutan invaded Sikkim and held that country for about six years (1700-6). In 1773, Bhutan intervened in the affairs of Cooch Behar. When the East India Company sent an expedition to Bhutan on behalf of Cooch Behar and captured Bhutanese territories, China did not figure in any way during the conflict. On 25 April 1774, the Government of Bhutan concluded a treaty of peace with the East India Company without making any reference to China or Tibet.

China's claim to suzerainty over Bhutan either directly or indirectly through its overlordship over Tibet has no basis in history. In fact, the history of British relations with Bhutan negates the claim. In 1841, the East India Company annexed the Assam Dooars of Bhutan. In 1864, the British Government of India declared war on Bhutan, annexed a large slice of Bhutan, and concluded a treaty of peace in 1865. In all the above wars, annexations, and treaties, the British dealt with Bhutan directly and without any reference to China. If China had been Bhutan's suzerain, it would not have been a silent spectator to foreign aggression on its vassal state. In fact, the Bhutanese authorities were supreme in the affairs of their state and foiled all attempts of the Chinese Amban and of the Tibetans to impose their authority on Bhutan.

Although King Ugyen Wangchuck did not acquiesce in China's claim to suzerainty over his kingdom, he realised that it was almost impossible to prevent Chinese expansionism over his kingdom without British protection. Hence the King signed a treaty with the British Government of India on 8 January 1910, by which Bhutan agreed to be guided by the advice of the British Government of India in regard to its external relations and the British Government of India undertook to exercise no interference in the internal affairs of Bhutan. However, China attempted to ignore the treaty of 1910, and claimed political supremacy over Bhutan. In June 1910, the Chinese Amban wrote to the King of Bhutan demanding an explanation from him for allowing some followers and the property of the Dalai Lama to pass through Bhutan. He also asked the Bhutanese ruler that the Chinese-Tibetan currency should be allowed to circulate in Bhutan. But the British Government of India rejected China's claim to suzerainty over Bhutan and insisted on the observance of the treaty of 1910. It considered itself bound to resist any attempt on the part of China to impose its authority on, or, in any way to interfere in Bhutan. Thus, the treaty of 1910 proved an effective tool to checkmate China's ambitions to establish its suzerainty over Bhutan.

Continuance of Hostile Relations Towards Bhutan by Communist China

In the post Second World War period Bhutan continued their stand-offish relations towards China. When the Communist Party of China came to power under the leadership of Mao Zedong in 1949, it took no steps to normalise its relations with Bhutan. As a matter of fact the Communist Government of China continued to follow the expansionist policy of Manchu emperors. As early as in 1930, Mao Zedong wrote that the correct boundary of China would include Burma, Bhutan, Nepal, Taiwan, Korea and Ryykyu islands.[7] Soon after establishing itself the Communist Government of China sent its People Liberation of Army to Tibet. The Chinese action in Tibet had a strong impact on the Bhutanese people who had close religious and cultural ties with the Tibetan people.

China took an antagonistic step against Bhutan in 1958, when it published maps which showed about 200 sq. miles of Bhutanese territory as part of Tibet. Chinese hostilities towards Bhutan came to the crunch in 1959, when the Chinese seized Bhutan's eight enclaves in western Tibet, which had been administered by Bhutan since the seventeenth century. The Chinese expelled the Bhutanese officials from the enclaves and took over them.[8] Moreover, the Bhutanese people were appalled at the ruthless suppression of Tibetan revolt by China, the flight of the Dalai Lama to India and the assemblage of Chinese troops near Bhutan's northern border in 1959. Consequently, the Government of Bhutan closed its border with Tibet. However, the Chinese started encroaching on Bhutanese pasture land in the 1960s. The Chinese encroachment on the Bhutanese territory used to be in the form of Tibetan graziers intruding into the Bhutanese pasture land. In the 1970s, the Tibetan incursions into the Bhutanese territory increased. Tibetan herdsmen intruded not only into the western sector of Bhutan, but also into the central sector. In 1979, the Tibetan incursions into the Bhutanese territory took place on a large scale. This incident led the Government of Bhutan to decide on entering into direct negotiations with China on the delineation and demarcation of the Bhutan-China boundary.

The Government of Bhutan established informal contact with the Chinese authorities in 1981, and held the first formal talks with China in Beijing on 17 April 1984. Between April 1981 and January 2010, nineteen rounds of boundary talks took place between Bhutan and China, but they have not been able to reach final agreement on their boundary dispute. Moreover, Tibetans continued incursions into the Bhutanese territory. They intruded not only into Doklam, Charithang, Sinchulumpa and Dramana in western sector, but also in Majathang and Jakarlung in the central sector of the boundary. In 1995, several members of the National Assembly of Bhutan expressed their concern that if the traditional Bhutanese pasture land were taken over by Tibetans, it would adversely affect the economic condition of Bhutanese yak herders. Hence the Government of Bhutan has been appealing to China that its traditional pasture land on which its yak herders depended for their livelihood be restored to them, but China is intent on retaining the Bhutanese territory because of its strategic importance. This is one of the main reasons why Bhutan has been disinclined to normalise its relations with China.

Bhutan's Partnership with India: Response to India's Friendship

While China has been intransigent on its boundary dispute with Bhutan, India has been taking measures to strengthen its friendship with the Himalayan Kingdom of Bhutan. Soon after India attained independence from the British rule, the Indian Government led by Prime Minister Jawaharlal Nehru decided to establish a new relationship with Bhutan, based on close friendship and good neighbourliness. Hence India and Bhutan concluded a new treaty on 8 August 1949, "to promote and foster the relations of friendship and neighbourliness so necessary for the wellbeing of their peoples." Under this treaty, the Government of India undertook to exercise no interference in the internal affairs of Bhutan. On its part the Government of Bhutan agreed to be guided by the advice of the Government of India in regard to its external relations. Moreover, India made a friendly gesture towards Bhutan by agreeing to return 32 square miles of territory in the Dewangiri district of Assam. The treaty also provided for free trade between India and Bhutan. India undertook to provide facilities for the carriage by land and water, of Bhutanese produce throughout its territory. The treaty gave Bhutan the right to import with the consent of India such arms, communication and machinery as may be needed for the defence and welfare of Bhutan. India also increased Bhutan's annual subsidy to Rupee five lakh.[9]

Bhutan's Emergence in the Comity of Nations and India's Role

India won the friendship and goodwill of the Kingdom of Bhutan largely by helping the Kingdom to acquire its due place in the comity of nations. Since China put an end to Tibet's autonomy in 1959, the Bhutanese people became keen to gain international recognition of the status of their country as a sovereign and independent nation. Hence they wanted to establish diplomatic relations with foreign countries. However, the late King Jigme Dorji Wangchuck was not in haste. Before establishing diplomatic relations with foreign countries, he wanted to bring about modern development in his Kingdom. He said, "We have at present no roads, no trade or industry. We must develop our state first." In the aftermath of the Sino-Indian war of 1962, which shook Bhutan's confidence in India's capability to protect it from Chinese aggression, it began to think of joining the United Nations.

India's response to Bhutanese aspirations was cautious but quite positive. Its policy has been to gradually broaden Bhutan's foreign relations which proved beneficial to the Kingdom without involving it in big power international politics. India sponsored Bhutan's membership of the Colombo Plan and a Bhutanese delegation participated as observer at the meeting of the Colombo Plan Consultative Committee in November 1962. Bhutan was admitted as a full member of the Council at its 17th session held in Colombo on 7 March 1963. Since then many members of the Colombo Plan provided economic and technical assistance to Bhutan.

Although the Kingdom of Bhutan wanted to become a member of the United Nations, it was not prepared to assume the responsibilities and obligations of the UN in the 1960s. In 1966, the Pakistani Press made propaganda that the Indian Government was strongly opposed to any Bhutanese attempt to join the UN, but the Pakistani propaganda had no effect on Bhutan-India friendship. On 5 June 1967, M. C. Chagla, the then Minister of External Affairs, stated in the Lok Sabha, "The Government of India would be happy to sponsor Bhutan for membership of the United Nations and other international bodies when Bhutan expresses its readiness to assume the responsibilities and obligations of such membership." Bhutan was not even member of the Universal Postal Union till 1967. In April 1967, India sponsored Bhutan's application for admission to the Union. Bhutan became a member of the Universal Postal Union in March 1969. By the year 1970, Bhutan became prepared to assume the responsibilities and obligations of the UN. India sponsored Bhutan's application for membership of the UN in December 1970. It also made every possible effort to canvass support among the member-nations of the UN for Bhutan's admission. On 7 February 1971, the Security Council unanimously recommended to the General Assembly Bhutan's application for admission to the UN. King Jigme Dorji Wangchuck visited New Delhi in April 1971. The visit was followed by the establishment of the Royal Bhutan Mission in New Delhi in May 1971. Bhutan's first representative in India, Lyonpo Pema Wangchuck presented his credentials to the President of India on 17 May 1971. India also appointed B.S. Das as its representative in Thimphu on 15 July 1971. On 21 September 1971, Bhutan became a full-fledged member of the UN. Prince Namgyal Wangchuck, leader of the Bhutanese delegation who addressed the General Assembly on 21 September 1971, on the occasion of the admission of Bhutan to the UN, thanked, on behalf of his King and the people of Bhutan, all members of the UN, and in particular India "which has spared no efforts in securing our admission to the UN." He also said, "this is a historic occasion for us and marks the realisation of one of our most cherished dreams."[10]

Possibly the Bhutanese desire for becoming a member of the UN would have remained an unfulfilled dream if Communist

China had entered the world body before Bhutan did. China would have used its veto against the admission of Bhutan to the UN, since the former looked upon the latter as an extension of Tibet. China had already declared in 1959 that it would "liberate" Bhutan and Sikkim in due course. However, Bhutan showed its foresight and statesmanship by voting in the UN on 25 October 1971, in favour of the Albanian resolution which sought to expel Nationalist China from the UN and admit Communist China to the UN.

Exchange of Goodwill Visits Between India and Bhutan

India has been willing to cultivate friendly relations with Bhutan by promoting exchange of goodwill visits between the two countries. The ball was set rolling by Prime Minister Jawaharlal Nehru who visited Bhutan in September 1958. The Prime Minister of India made it clear in his speech in Bhutan that India's only desire for the Kingdom of Bhutan was that it should remain independent and choose its own direction and progress. Prime Minister Nehru's visit was followed by a delegation of five members of the Indian Parliament, which visited Bhutan in October 1967. King Jigme Dorji Wangchuck visited India in February 1961 and in April 1966. A seven-member delegation of the Royal Advisory Council of Bhutan paid a goodwill visit to India in December 1967. In March 1968, Morarji Desai, the then Deputy Prime Minister of India, paid a goodwill visit to Bhutan. In May 1968, Indira Gandhi, the then Prime Minister of India visited Bhutan. King Jigme Dorji Wangchuck welcoming her described the bonds of friendship between India and Bhutan as being such "that nothing can ever shake or destroy." Prime Minister Indira Gandhi said India wanted the Kingdom of Bhutan to develop its own system based on its rich culture and heritage. During this visit the Indian Prime Minister inaugurated the 127-mile Phuntsoling-Thimphu Highway, a major Indo-Bhutanese cooperation project which links the capital of Bhutan with its principal trade and commercial town near the Indo-Bhutanese border. Prime Minister Indira Gandhi also laid the foundation stone of Bharat Bhavan (India House) which accommodates the office and residence of Indian ambassador in Bhutan.

Besides the exchanges of visits of representatives of the two governments who often met and discussed matters of mutual interest, cultural and educational trips have also been frequently arranged between India and Bhutan. A twenty-member delegation of Bhutanese lamas visited places of Buddhist pilgrimage in India in January 1967. A fifteen-member troupe of the Kathak Kala Kendra from New Delhi visited Bhutan in March 1967 and gave performances which were greatly appreciated. A group of 40 Bhutanese school boys visited India on Bharat Darshan from 14 January to 12 February 1968. A Bhutanese cultural troupe visited New Delhi in January 1969 and took part in the Folk Dance Festival.

India's friendly relations with Bhutan were highlighted by the state visit of V. V. Giri, the then President of India, to Bhutan in April 1970. Welcoming the President, the King of Bhutan said that the visit was a historic event, not only because it was the first time that an Indian Head of the State was visiting Bhutan, but also because it was a proof of strong bonds of goodwill and friendship between the two countries. President Giri said that India and Bhutan were not merely two neighbouring countries but very close friends sharing a common heritage and understanding throughout history. The ties of friendship between India and Bhutan were further strengthened by the exchange of various delegations. A 16-member Indian folk dance troupe visited in August 1971. Five delegations from Bhutan, each consisting of a separate group of persons such as members of the National Assembly, members of the Royal Advisory Council, officials, students, teachers and artists visited India in January-February 1972.

India-Bhutan friendship which was strengthened by Prime Minister Indira Gandhi was consolidated by Prime Minister Rajiv Gandhi. He cultivated personal friendship with King Jigme Singye Wangchuck and visited Bhutan in 1985 and 1988. He reaffirmed India's commitment to Bhutan's economic development. During this period India's involvement in Bhutan's development programme began to be considered as sharing of resources for common benefit of the two countries. In 1988, President R. Venkataraman visited Bhutan and inaugurated the Chukha Hydroelectric Project. The project had been set up by India at a cost of about Rs 2460 million, 60 per cent of the sum was a grant made by India and the rest a loan. Since 1986 the Chukha Project started its generation of electricity and Bhutan began exporting electricity to India.

P. V. Narasimha Rao who became the Prime Minister of India in 1990, took steps to further strengthen friendship with Bhutan. He visited Bhutan in August 1993, and his talks with the King of Bhutan in Thimphu covered the increased economic cooperation between the two countries.[11]

King Jigme Singye Wangchuck also played a very important role in strengthening Bhutan-India friendship. He visited India several times and consolidated Bhutan's relations with India. India-Bhutan friendship was further strengthened during the premiership of Manmohan Singh (2004-2014). India updated the Friendship Treaty of 1949 in 2007.[12] Some Bhutanese were averse to Article 2 of the 1949 treaty which provided that Bhutan would be guided by the advice of the Government of India in regard to its external relations. Hence the updating of the Friendship Treaty in 2007 further strengthened Bhutan's relations with India. Moreover, Prime Minister Manmohan Singh visited Bhutan on 16 May 2008, and said, "India stands ready to join hands with the people and the Government of Bhutan to further strengthen our relationship and do our bit for accelerated development of Bhutan."[13]

King Jigme Singye Wangchuck abdicated in 2006, and his son and successor, Jigme Khesar Namgyel Wangchuck acceded to the Bhutanese throne. King Jigme Khesar Namgyel Wangchuck regards himself "as the staunchest proponent of Indo-Bhutan friendship." He visited India several times. In January 2013, the Government of India invited the King to visit India as the Chief Guest at the 64th Republic Day celebrations in New Delhi. The King accepted the invitation and offered his "deepest, most profound affection and goodwill to the people of India" on the occasion of the Republic Day celebration. He observed that his "bond with India is for life."[14]

India-Bhutan Partnership in Economic Development

India has been able to gain Bhutan's friendship on account of its diverse efforts, but its partnership in economic development is one of the main factors which forged Bhutan-India friendship. Since 1961, when the Royal Government of Bhutan embarked on the economic development of the Kingdom, India has been the major donor of aid for Bhutan's economic development. India's economic aid to Bhutan has already been dealt with in the preceding chapter. Therefore, the repetition may be avoided for that reason.

Besides providing financial aid for Bhutan's developmental plans, India has been helping the Kingdom to promote and diversify its trade. Being a land-locked country, Bhutan's trade with third countries was to be conducted through the Indian territory. Hence in 1983, India and Bhutan signed a trade agreement which provided not only free trade between the two countries but also transit facilities to Bhutan for the conduct of trade with the third countries. According to the trade agreement signed on 02 March 1990, free trade between the two countries continued as heretofore. Moreover, India and Bhutan signed an agreement on trade, commerce and transit in New Delhi 28 July 2006. They agreed that there would, as heretofore, be free trade and commerce between the two countries. However, the Government of Bhutan may henceforth impose such non-tariff restrictions on the entry into Bhutan of certain goods of Indian origin as may be necessary for the protection of industries in Bhutan. Such restrictions, however, will not be stricter than those applied to goods of the origin of third countries. In recent years, India-Bhutan partnership increased in building hydropower projects. The hydropower has been Bhutan's main export to India, accounting for 25.7 per cent of its exports, earning Rs 3.4 billion in 2005.

India-Bhutan friendship entered on high when the NDA Government led by Prime Minister Narendra Modi took office in New Delhi in May 2014. Prime Minister Modi gave priority to improving relations with the neighbouring countries and invited all Heads of Governments of the SAARC countries to his swearing-in ceremony. Moreover, Prime Minister Modi paid goodwill visit to Bhutan on 15 June 2014, Prime Minister Modi's first visit abroad after taking over office of Prime Minister. Prime Minister Modi described Bhutan as a natural choice for his first visit abroad as the two countries shared a "special relationship."

Prime Minister Modi laid the foundation stone of the 600 MW Kholongchu hydropower project. He said, "our hydropower cooperation is a classic example of win-win cooperation and a model for the entire region." Prime Minister Modi also inaugurated the Supreme Court building which has been built with Indian assistance.

Prime Minister Modi addressed the joint sitting of Bhutan's Parliament on 16 June 2014. He pledged that India would assist Bhutan in setting up a digital library which would provide access to the Bhutanese youth to two million books and periodicals. He said that educational links were important for strengthening people-to-people contacts. He announced the doubling of the Nehru-Wangchuck scholarship to Rs 20 million per year. He said that the Government of India would also provide assistance for the establishment of the digital library in the National Library of Bhutan and in all 20 districts of Bhutan. Prime Minister Modi reiterated the commitment of the Government of India to support Bhutan for the successful implementation of the 11th Five Year Plan of the Royal Government of Bhutan. India pledged to provide Rs 45 billion for the 11th Five Year Plan and Rs 5 billion for the economic stimulus plan of the Royal Government of Bhutan.

In his meeting with King Jigme Khesar Namgyel Wangchuck and Prime Minister Tshering Togay, Prime Minister Modi described India's bilateral ties with Bhutan as "B2B relations – Bharat to Bhutan relations." The two sides exchanged views and held discussions on bilateral relations and economic cooperation as well as cooperation in regional and multilateral forums. They recalled the strong historical ties of friendship and understanding that exist between the governments and peoples of the two countries. They expressed satisfaction at the excellent state of bilateral relations and reaffirmed their commitment to further strengthen the special friendship between the two countries. The two sides also expressed satisfaction with the cooperation between the two countries related to their mutual security. They agreed to continue with their close coordination and cooperation with each other on issues relating to their national interests, and not allow each other's territory to be used for interest inimical to other.[15]

The visit of Prime Minister Modi to Bhutan further strengthened the close bonds of friendship and cooperation between India and the Kingdom of Bhutan.

References

1. Ram Rahul, "Making of Modern Bhutan," in International Studies, Vol.19, No. 3, July-September1980, pp. 515-28.
2. The Tibetans belong to the Gelukpa school of Lamaism.
3. Ram Rahul, No. 1.
4. Kapileshwar Labh, "China as a Factor in the Policy of British India Towards Nepal," in Journal of Indian History, Trivandrum, Vol. 55, December 1977, pp.177-88.
5. Kapileshwar Labh, India and Bhutan, New Delhi, 1974, pp.167-69.
6. L. Oppenheim, International Law: A Treatise, London, 1928, edn. 4, Vol. 1, p.186.
7. Dalip Mehta, "India and Bhutan," in Atish Sinha and Madhup Mehta, ed., Indian Foreign Policy: Challenges and Opportunities, New Delhi, 2007, p. 576.

   See also Parmanand, The Politics of Bhutan: Retrospect and Prospect, Delhi, 1992, p.163.
8. Leo E. Rose, The Politics of Bhutan, New York, 1977, p. 80.
9. Kapileshwar Labh, no. 5, pp. 221-25.
10. *Ibid.*
11. Times of India, New Delhi, 23 August 1993.
12. Avtar Singh Bhasin, ed., India's Foreign Relations-2006 Documents, New Delhi, 2007, pp. 714-16.
13. *Ibid.*, 17 May 2008.
14. *Ibid.*, 16 June 2014.
15. P M Narendra Modi-Bhutan: Website.

10

Role of Political Institutions in Bhutan's Foreign Policy Decision-Making Process

The Bhutanese ruling elite not only brought about economic development in their country but also raised the Kingdom of Bhutan's standing in the comity of nations by adopting peaceful and friendly relations with almost all countries of the world. Hence it would be apt to study the role of Bhutan's political institutions in its foreign policy decision-making process.

This chapter includes the study of role of the Monarchy, the National Assembly, the Royal Advisory Council, the Ministry of Foreign Affairs, and of pressure groups such as business interests, armed forces, civil servants in the foreign policy decision-making process of Bhutan.

The Role of Monarchy

The monarchy has been pivotal in the political system of Bhutan. Prior to 1972, when Dawa Tsering was appointed Foreign Minister of Bhutan, the Bhutanese kings themselves played the role of foreign ministers of their Kingdom. King Ugyen Wangchuck (1907-26), the first King of Bhutan, took vital decisions on his Kingdom's foreign policy. In 1910, he threw in his Kingdom's lot with British India in view of looming China's threats to Bhutan's independence: he signed a treaty with British India by which he agreed to be guided by British India in regard to Bhutan's external affairs, and British India on its part pledged not to interfere in the internal affairs of Bhutan. The second King, Jigme Wangchuck (1926-52), who consolidated peace and security in the country, renewed Bhutan's relations with India by signing a treaty of perpetual peace and friendship on 8 August 1949.

The third King, Jigme Dorji Wangchuck (1952-72), played a decisive role in reorienting Bhutan's foreign policy. He was an enlightened and far-sighted ruler. He felt that Bhutan's isolationist policy was not beneficial for the country and he opened up his Kingdom to the outside world. However, his approach to foreign policy was based on the assumption that India would permit Bhutan a cautious and progressive diversification of its foreign relations, if this would not harm India's interest. During his rule Bhutan joined the Colombo Plan (1962), the Universal Postal Union (1969), and the UN (1971). Moreover, he opened a new chapter in Bhutan-India relations by establishing Royal Bhutan Mission in New Delhi in May 1971. Bhutan became an important member of the comity of nations. King Jigme Dorji Wangchuck is regarded as the architect of modern Bhutan.[1]

The fourth King, Jigme Singye Wangchuck, occupies a special place among the Bhutanese monarchs. The Bhutanese people believe that King Jigme Singye Wangchuck is "a sacred reincarnate destined to safeguard the nation and take care of his people." Born on 11 November 1955, he had his early education in India, the UK and at the Ugyen Wangchuck Academy at Paro. In May 1972, Prince Jigme Singye Wangchuck was appointed the Tongsa Penlop. When King Jigme Dorji Wangchuck died, the Prince was crowned at a young age of 17 on 22 July 1972.

King Jigme Singye Wangchuck played principal role in formulating the foreign policy of the Kingdom. He granted audiences to most of the foreign missions visiting Bhutan, and acquainted them with his foreign policy. He addressed SAARC and Non-Aligned Summits and proclaimed the Kingdom's regional and global policy. Since the inception of SAARC the King participated in SAARC Summit meetings and spoke not only on the need to improve bilateral political relations and increase economic cooperation between the SAARC countries, but also on the issues of terrorism, drug trafficking and the need for creating the SAARC food security reserve. The King spoke on the increasing menace of terrorism at the Colombo SAARC Summit on 21 December 1991, and stressed the need to "work together to eradicate this menace before it engulfs our societies and tears our nations apart." He expressed concern over the increasing nuclear arms proliferation in South Asia and stressed the need of elimination of all nuclear weapons from the region.

King Jigme Singye Wangchuck participated in Non-Aligned Summit meetings and endeavoured to strengthen the Non-Aligned Movement by emphasising "the essence of Non-Aligned Movement" which according to him consisted in the "rejection of all forms of subjugation, dependence, interference and intervention." He set store by the economic dimension of non-aligned movement which, he said, could not be relegated to the background. He laid emphasis by saying that " it must be accorded priority, and allowed to assume prominence in our deliberations."[2]

In the Non-Aligned Summit conferences King Jigme Singye Wangchuck supported the freedom struggles of peoples who were under foreign rule. At the Harrare Summit in 1986, the King said that the Kingdom of Bhutan had supported the people of Zimbabwe during the dark days of their liberation movement. He said that the choice of Harrare as the venue of the summit had a special significance for the Non-Aligned Movement. He said that it was "an expression of our solidarity with the peoples of South Africa and Nambia in their struggles for equality and freedom." The King also supported the struggles of Palestinian people. He said, "We remain firm in our stand that rights of the Palestinians under the leadership of PLO must be fully restored, including the right to self-determination in their homeland."[3]

King Jigme Singye Wangchuck drew attention to the international economic crisis. He expressed disappointment that the developing countries were still far from achieving a New International Economic Order, despite repeated calls by the previous Non-Aligned Summits for global negotiations and North-South Cooperation. He emphasised the need to revive the north-south dialogue in a spirit of mutual understanding and meaningful cooperation. He held that the developed countries must recognise the truly integrated and interdependent nature of the global economy and accept their responsibilities as the stronger partners in the international economic order. He also stressed the importance of South-South Cooperation and cooperation among members of Non-Aligned Movement as a means to enhance their economic potential and strengthen their collective bargaining power in North-South negotiations. The King held the view that a committed and coordinated stand on economic issues by the Non-Aligned Movement in the UN and other international forums would give an impetus to their efforts to bring about the establishment of a New International Economic Order.

King Jigme Singye Wangchuck emphasised the need of general and complete disarmament at the Belgrade Non-Aligned Summit in 1989. He welcomed the dramatic breakthrough by the two Super Powers on the issue of nuclear arms reduction, but he deplored the massive military expenditures incurred by many developing countries at the cost of basic human needs. The King called upon all countries to cut back such expenditures and he urged the Super Powers to maintain the momentum of their dialogue and to take further steps towards the elimination of all nuclear weapons.

The King urged the non-aligned countries to transcend the narrow differences that divided them and to use the opportunity provided by the Belgrade Summit to impart a renewed sense of purpose and direction to the Non-Aligned Movement. For his part, the King reaffirmed Bhutan's commitment to the goals and principles of the Non-Aligned Movement.[4]

Bhutan witnessed significant political change in the first decade of the twenty first century. King Jigme Singye Wangchuck abdicated in December 2006, and was succeeded by his son Jigme Khesar Namgyel Wangchuck. In 2008, Bhutan adopted the first written Constitution under which Bhutan became a democratic constitutional monarchy. The King is the Head of State, and the Cabinet headed by Prime Minister would aid and advise the King in the exercise of his functions including international affairs.

King Jigme Khesar Namgyel Wangchuck whose coronation was celebrated in 2008, became the fifth King of Bhutan. The King by and large follows in his father's footsteps in sphere of his country's foreign policy. He visited India on a number of occasions and strengthened relations with India. The King pursues policy of peace and friendship with all countries of the world.

Role of the National Assembly

In 1953, the third King, Jigme Dorji Wangchuck established the Tshogdu (the National Assembly) which was regarded as the parliament of Bhutan. The National Assembly consisted of 154 members belonging to three categories: 105 elected representatives of the people, 12 representatives of the clergy and 37 nominated representatives of the Royal Government. The members of the National Assembly had complete freedom of speech and could discuss and pass resolutions on any subject. They evinced their interest in the foreign affairs of their country.

In May 1960, the members of the National Assembly of Bhutan raised the issue of the Bhutan-India boundary as shown in maps published by the Indian Government in its White Paper on relations with China.The error in maps was pointed out in a letter to the Government of India mentioning that the Bhutan-India boundary had been shown by a thin line as if that line separated Indian states. Bhutan demanded that the line should be marked thicker and in deeper colour so as to look like an international boundary. The members of National Assembly who were mostly sensitive about the sovereign status of their country wanted the Bhutan-India boundary be shown clearly as an international boundary by India. The Indian Government clarified the position stating that the Bhutanese protest was based on a misunderstanding. It pointed out that the map was enlargement from a standard map of India prepared by the Survey of India in which Bhutan had been shown in yellow colour which signified a distinct status for Bhutan, but the map attached to the White Paper was in black and white. Therefore, the distinct colour of the line could not be reproduced in that particular map.[5]

The members of National Assembly also expressed their concern over Bhutan-China border dispute. They said that since the Bhutanese people living in the northern region mostly depended on the income from their yaks, the loss of the grazing ground would mean the loss of their livelihood. They expressed their anxieties that if the traditional Bhutanese boundary was altered, it would adversely affect the economy of the yak herders of the country. They requested the Government of Bhutan to ensure that the northern boundary be properly demarcated.[6]

The members of National Assembly also called upon the government to discontinue the bilateral talks with Nepal on the issue of Bhutanese refugees staying in eastern Nepal. In July 1993, Bhutan and Nepal established a Ministerial-level Joint Committee to resolve the dispute. Since October 1993, seven rounds of talks had taken place between Bhutan and Nepal but the two countries could not resolve the refugee issue. There were indeed wide differences between Nepal and Bhutan over the issue. While the former wanted to repatriate all refugees to Bhutan, the latter was inclined to accept only those bona fide Bhutanese citizens who had been forcibly evicted from Bhutan.

The members of National Assembly from Haa, Peme Gatshel and other districts said that the Joint Ministerial Committee had made good progress in the first five rounds of talks, but Nepal suddenly changed its stand later on and all the past agreements had become meaningless. The representative from the Dorokha district observed that there was no point to continue the Bhutan-Nepal talks because there was no progress. He contended that the talks should be discontinued because Nepal's stand changed every time when there was a change in the government of Nepal. He pointed out that Nepal's new stand was that Bhutan should take back all the refugees who had lived in Bhutan whether they were Bhutanese citizens or not, and the verification of their claims to be genuine Bhutanese refugees was to be based on their individual statement. Thus, several members of National Assembly expressed their opposition to the continuation of talks with Nepal on the refugee issue.[7]

Role of the Royal Advisory Council

In 1965, King Jigme Dorji Wangchuck established the Lodey Tshogdey (the Royal Advisory Council) which consisted of nine members: six representatives of the people, two representatives of the clergy and one nominee of the King. The main functions of the Royal Advisory Council were to advise the King on all matters of national concern and to promote the welfare of Bhutanese people and the national interest of the Kingdom. King Jigme Singye Wangchuck enhanced the power and position of the Royal Advisory Council in 1984, when he got a special clause included in its rules and regulations which empowered it to report to the Cabinet and the National Assembly, as might be appropriate, in the event the action of any citizen or person including the King, was likely to cause harm to the country and its people.[8]

The Royal Advisory Council was primarily responsible to promote and safeguard the trust, confidence and the harmonious relations existing between the government and the people of the Kingdom. In this regard, if the council or anyone of its members became aware of situations or threats that might undermine the security, peace and stability of the Kingdom, such information was to be immediately brought to the attention of the King. The Royal Advisory Council was the "guardian" of the policies, laws and resolutions passed by the National Assembly and it ensured their faithful implementation by the government and the people. It endeavoured to ascertain whether the national policies, plans and programmes were being implemented by the government and the people. If it found out that they were not implemented, it brought the matter to the attention of the King. The Royal Advisory Councillors usually extended support to the Royal Government during the regular Cabinet meetings chaired by King to deliberate and decide upon actions to be taken in connection with resolving the anti-national problem. In 1990-91, when some ethnic Nepalese rose against the Royal Government in southern Bhutan, the Royal Advisory councillors from southern Bhutan accompanied the King during his visits to southern districts to restore peace and stability. Similarly, when the King made goodwill visits to northen and eastern districts, the concerned councillors accompanied the Royal entourage. Moreover, the Royal Advisory Council also discharged its responsibilities as an appellate authority under Bhutan's judicial system.[9]

Role of Prime Minister

Prior to the creation of office of Prime Ministers, the Bhutanese Agents in India acted more or less as Prime Ministers of Bhutan, who used to advise the Bhutanese Kings on Bhutan's foreign policy. Ugyen Dorji, known also as Ugyen Kazi was Bhutanese Agent in India during the reign of King Ugyen Wangchuck (1907-26). He played an important role in bringing about a close understanding between the Bhutanese and the British Indian authorities. It is noteworthy that Ugyen Dorji was instrumental in negotiating the treaty of 1910 between Bhutan and British India. Ugyen Dorli died in 1916, and was succeeded by his son, Sonam Tobgay Dorji as Bhutanese Agent in India. Sonam T. Dorji followed in his father's footsteps with regard to Bhutan's foreign policy. When King Ugyen Wangchuck died on 21 August 1926, and was succeeded by his son, Jigme Wangchuck, Sonam T. Dorji became the chief advisor of the King on the country's foreign policy. Under his stewardship Bhutan continued to maintain friendly relations with India, and signed a Treaty of Friendship with India on 8 August 1949. However, Bhutan continued to follow a close-door policy in order to preserve its way of life and its autonomy.[10]

Jigmie Dorji who succeeded his father, Sonam T. Dorji, was officially designated as Prime Minister of Bhutan in 1958 at the time of the visit of Prime Minister Jawaharlal Nehru to Bhutan. As King Jigme Dorji Wangchuck (1952-72) focused his time and energy on domestic affairs, Prime Minister Jigmie Dorji mainly looked after the Kingdom's foreign affairs.

Bhutan faced a critical period in its foreign relations in the late 1950s when China unleashed terror and repression in Tibet. Many Tibetans fled their country, infiltrated into Bhutan and narrated the atrocities perpetrated by Chinese troops on Tibetans. The flight of the Dalai Lama to India and assemblage of Chinese troops near Bhutan's northern border alarmed the Bhutanese. Prime Minister Jigmie Dorji could not remain indifferent to such a situation. He visited India in August 1959, and sought Indian support in the event of a Chinese attack on Bhutan.

The career of Prime Minister Jigmie Dorji was cut short by his assassination in 1964. He was succeeded by his brother,

Lhendup Dorji, but the latter had to give up his post and go into exile in Nepal in 1965 owing to the factional politics of Bhutan. Hence King Jigme Dorji Wangchuck himself assumed the responsibility of Prime Minister.[11] In 1998, King Jigme Singye Wangchuck started a new system of governance in the kingdom by the elected cabinet. The Chairman of cabinet acted as Prime Minister of the country, represented Bhutan at the regional and international forums and played an important role in the Kingdom's foreign policy decision-making process. Jigme Thinley became the first Chairman of the Cabinet of Bhutan. Sangay Ngedup succeeded him and took over as Chairman and Head of the Government on 16 August 1999.[12]

The office of Prime Minister was revived in 2008, when the general election took place in Bhutan, and Jigme Thinley, the leader of the Druk Phuensum Tshogpa (DPT) won larger number of seats (44 out of 47 seats) in the National Assembly, and became the first democratically elected Prime Minister of Bhutan. Prime Minister Jigme Thinley maintained friendly relations with all countries. He, however, endeavoured to bring a change in the country's foreign policy. He expanded Bhutan's diplomatic relations from 21 to 53 countries between 2008 and 2013.[13] In July 2013, when the second general election took place in Bhutan, the People's Democratic Party (PDP), headed by Tshering Tobgay won majority of seats (32 seats out of 47) in the National Assembly. Tshering Tobgay became the Prime Minister of Bhutan in July 2013. Under his leadership Bhutan has been following policy of peace and goodwill towards all nations, while being "mindful" of its geographical realities.[14]

Role of the Ministry of Foreign Affairs

Among the Foreign Ministers who headed Bhutan's Foreign Ministry, the name of Dawa Tsering stands out. He was born on 29 September 1935. He obtained the Degrees of Bachelor of Arts in 1956, and Bachelor of Law in 1959 from the University of

Calcutta. He was appointed Director of Education in 1960. In 1969, he was appointed as Bhutan's first Minister of Planning and Development, and in 1970, given the additional portfolio of the newly created Ministry of Foreign Affairs. In 1972, he was appointed full-time Minister for Foreign Affairs, in which capacity he continued to serve till 1998. Thus, he became the longest serving Foreign Minister of Bhutan.

Dawa Tsering played a significant role in making of Bhutan's foreign policy. He led Bhutanese delegations to the UN, Non-aligned meetings, ESCAP, UNCTAD, and articulated Bhutan's world-views at international forums. He reaffirmed his country's commitment to the ideals of the UN Charter and the principles of non-alignment. He condemned the prevalence of colonialism and racism, and emphasised the need of disarmament for maintenance of peace in the world. He stressed the need of reform in the UN, and pleaded that the Security Council should be expanded to allow greater representation of developing countries. In this context he strongly supported India's candidature for a permanent seat on the Security Council. He highlighted the economic hardship of the least developed and landlocked countries, and pleaded for substantial economic aid for least developed landlocked countries.

Dawa Tsering strove to strengthen his country's relations with India. He held that the friendship with India was the cornerstone of Bhutan's foreign policy. He said that "for a small and landlocked country like Bhutan, a close relationship with India is vital for its survival as a nation and for the well-being of its people."[15] Dawa Tsering also took initiatives in starting talks with China on Bhutan-China boundary dispute in 1984. The Royal Government of Bhutan held 10 rounds of talks with the Chinese Government by 1995. Foreign Minister Dawa Tsering led the Bhutanese delegation in the talks. During the first five rounds the Bhutanese delegation along with the Chinese worked out the guiding principles under which the talks were to be conducted. In the following five rounds they were able to make steady progress in harmonising the issues related to the demarcation of the Bhutan-China boundary.[16]

In 1998, when Jigme Y. Thinley was one of elected cabinet ministers, he was appointed as Foreign Minister of Bhutan. He made significant contributions to the making of Bhutan's foreign policy. He addressed the 53rd session of the UN General Assembly. In his address he pleaded for complete elimination of nuclear and all other weapons of mass destruction. Jigme Y. Thinley said that while the nuclear tests then conducted in South Asia had caused much concern, the steps taken by the concerned countries, viz., India and Pakistan, to allay the fears of the international community were heartening. Moreover, the Foreign Minister of Bhutan strongly recommended the inclusion of India and Japan as permanent members of the Security Council, and appealed to the international community to help Bangladesh in the aftermath of then flood. He also highlighted the political reforms introduced by King Jigme Singye Wangchuck in his Kingdom. He said that the political reforms brought in by the King had enhanced the direct participation of the people in his country's development and governance.

Jigme Y. Thinley signed an agreement with his Chinese counterpart during the 12th round of Bhutan-China talks in Beijing on 8 December 1998. Under the agreement the two countries agreed to observe the status quo of the Bhutan-China boundary. The agreement brought about peace on Bhutan's northern border.[17]

Khandu Wangchuck who succeeded Jigme Y. Thinley followed in his predecessor's footsteps in the sphere of his country's foreign policy. He also advocated the policy of peace and friendship with all countries. He addressed the 58th session of UN General Assembly and emphasised the need for peace, security and poverty alleviation.[18]

Role of the Army and the Civil Servants

In some countries the army and civil servants play an important role in their countries' foreign policy decision-making process. Hence it is worthwhile to study their role in Bhutan.

In Bhutan there was no standing army until the mid-1950s. During the period of Shabdrung rule Bhutanese Chiefs maintained their separate forces consisting of untrained village conscripts. In the event of war, Bhutan could raise around 10,000 men, and an Arrow Chief (Dapon) was appointed to command all Bhutanese forces consisting of the various private units of the Bhutanese Chiefs. Although the Bhutanese forces were almost untrained and without modern weapons, they could fight their enemies with courage and determination which they demonstrated during the 1864-65 war with the British. Under the monarchy there was no immediate change in the organisation of Bhutan's military force. The Dzongpons in districts maintained a small militia who functioned more as a police force rather than as a military force. There was a Royal Body Guard stationed at the palace, but this was an untrained force. It was only during the Second World War, when the Royal Body Guard was given some training and, provided with modern weapons. Moreover, a number of Bhutanese volunteered for service in the British Indian Army during the Second World War, two of whom were commissioned as officers.

In 1952, when the third King, Jigme Dorji Wangchuck succeeded to the throne, he decided to organise a standing army in the Kingdom. Several Bhutanese were sent to India for training in the British Indian army. These men returned to Bhutan on completion of their training, and one of them became the first brigadier of the Royal Bhutan Army. In 1955, King Jigme Dorji Wangchuck decided to strengthen the Royal Bhutan Army. There were two main reasons for this decision. First, the Chinese invaded Tibet in 1950-51, and they gradually expanded their control along the Tibet-Bhutan border. Besides, a major rebellion against the Chinese took place in Kham (eastern Tibet) in 1954, which caused a grave concern to the Bhutanese, and strengthened their resolve to reinforce the military force to defend their border. Second, the Nepali Bhutanese had launched a political movement against the Royal Government of Bhutan in 1948-54. The movement failed to make a headway but the Bhutanese realised that they needed an adequate military force to maintain internal security of the country.[19]

Initially Bhutan was disinclined to seek India's assistance in organising and training its military force. But by 1961, Bhutan's northern environment had assumed such a "threatening proportion" that the Bhutanese ruling elite could not avoid Indian assistance in training and equipping its army. In August 1962, an Indian Military Training Team (IMTRAT) was sent to Bhutan to assist in organising Bhutanese Officer's Training Centre at Ha Dzong in western Bhutan. Thus, the Royal Bhutan Army began to develop fast. By 1964, the size of Royal Bhutan Army rose to around 9,000 strong. But it became politicized before long. It involved itself in the politics of the Kingdom. Some army officers led by Brigadier Chabda Namgyal Bahadur, the then Chief of the Royal Bhutan Army became averse to the policy pursued by Prime Minister Jigmie Dorji, and decided to eliminate him. On 5 April 1964, when King Jigme Dorji Wangchuck happened to be away in Switzerland undergoing a medical treatment, the Prime Minister of Bhutan was assassinated at Phuntsholing on the Bhutan-India border by a non-commissioned officer of the Royal Bhutan Army.[20]

There are differences of opinion among scholars of Bhutanese affairs over the issue of assassination of Prime Minister Jigmie Dorji. Leo E. Rose considered the 1964 crisis more of a struggle for power within the political elite than any conflict over the Kingdom's policy.[21] But other scholars held that the change in Bhutan's policy was at the root of the assassination of the Prime Minister. Nari Rustomji wrote that the policy and programmes adopted by Jigmie Dorji alarmed the traditional groups particularly Buddhist lamas. He added that besides the lamas, there were other sections of the traditional group, particularly the old-timers in the Bhutanese army and civil service who were apprehensive that their vested interests would be endangered by Jigmie Dorji's development programmes and were hostile to Jigmie Dorji.[22] Ram Rahul wrote that the reforms and innovations did not go down well with old guards who decided to act by assassinating the man most closely identified with new changes. Indeed Jigmie Dorji had played an important role in ending the Kingdom's isolationist policy and launching the process of development programmes in Bhutan with India's aid and cooperation.[23]

King Jigme Dorji Wangchuck returned to Bhutan immediately on hearing the news of assassination of the Prime Minister. The Brigadier was arrested and tried on 16 May and executed on the following day. The King delegated power to Lhendup Dorji, Jigmie Dorji's younger brother, for civil administration. He handed over control over the army to his half-brother, Namgyal Wangchuck. King Jigme Dorji Wangchuck, however, resumed control over the army in 1968, and his son, Jigme Singye Wangchuck, held that control on accession to the throne in 1972. King Jigme Singye Wangchuck abdicated the throne and handed over his power as Monarch and Head of State to his son, Jigme Khesar Namgyel Wangchuck on 9 December 2006. The Constitution of Bhutan which was put into effect in 2008, stipulated that the executive power of the country would be vested in the Cabinet headed by the Prime Minister. Since the 1964 crisis the Royal Bhutan Army has kept away from the politics of the country and has been serving the King and the people of Bhutan with loyalty and dedication.

Role of Civil Servants

In several countries senior members of Civil Service especially those belonging to the ministry of foreign affairs play an important role in making of their countries' foreign policy.

Prior to the establishment of hereditary monarchy in 1907, the political system of Bhutan differed from that of other countries. The early Shabdrung rule in Bhutan was theocratic. Buddhist lamas were first in rank and first in power. There was no civil service in terms of its modern concept, nor was the ministry of foreign affairs. The Shabdrung succeeded himself by reincarnation, and the Deb Raja was elected by a council of lamas. The Deb Raja himself a lama was bound to consult monks on issues of war and peace. With the passage of time the Government of Bhutan became more feudalistic than theocratic. The Deb Raja who used to be elected by the State Council earlier, became merely a nominee of the powerful Ponlops. The foundation of hereditary monarchy in 1907, constituted a major change involving a shift towards the centralisation of political and administrative power. However, it did not lead to the expansion of official staff of the Kingdom's central administration. During the reign of the first two Kings, the Kingdom's central secretariat was small enough to be run from a room in the Royal palace at Bumthang.

In 1961, when the third King, King Jigme Dorji Wangchuck, embarked upon the political and economic development of Bhutan, it became essential to create a trained and efficient civil service. A new administrative structure was constructed at Tashichhodzong in Thimphu. With the creation of a council of ministers, the number of civil servants increased. In 1972, civil service rules were introduced about the appointment and promotion of civil servants. One of the rules laid down that all appointments and promotions would be made on a merit basis in which the educational qualifications and work records of civil servants would be given due consideration.[24] By 2010, the number of civil servants rose to around 24000 strong, and an independent and apolitical Civil Service Commission was established.[25]

Prior to 2008, there was no party politics in Bhutan. In the absence of political leaders, it was civil servants whose opinions on foreign policy issues were valued by the Bhutanese rulers. Thus, Bhutan's civil servants played an important role in foreign policy decision-making process.

Role of Pressure Groups

With the introduction of reforms and implementation of development programmes in Bhutan, there arose different groups such as farmers, businessmen, haves and have-nots, besides the army and the civil servants.

Among pressure groups businessmen were well organised, and they established the Bhutan Chamber of Commerce. The representatives of Bhutan Chamber of Commerce urged the Government of Bhutan not only to take steps to boost the country's foreign trade but also expressed concern that if the Bhutan-China boundary was demarcated as per the Chinese position, it would cause great problems and hardship for those people whose livelihood was dependent on grazing land for their yaks. They asked the government to ensure that Bhutan-China boundary was demarcated according to its traditional line.[26]

References

1. Kapileshwar Labh, India and Bhutan, New Delhi, 1974, pp. 223-25.
2. Text of the King's speech at the Non-Aligned Summit Conference, New Delhi, 7-11 March 1983.
3. Text of the King's speech at the Non-Aligned Summit Conference, Harrare, in September 1986.
4. Text of the King's speech at the Non-Aligned Summit Conference, Belgrade, in September 1989.
5. Ravi Verma, India's Role in the Emergence of Contemporary Bhutan, Delhi, 1988, p. 189.

6. Kuensel, 26 August 1995.
7. *Ibid*, 6 July 1996.
8. Kapileshwar Labh, "Political Development of Bhutan: Emerging Trends" in Ramakant and R. C. Misra, ed., Bhutan: Society and Polity, New Delhi, 1996, p. 206.
9. Kuensel, 29 August 1992.
10. Kapileshwar Labh, n.1, pp. 194-200.
11. Leo E. Rose, The Politics of Bhutan, New York, 1977, p.121.
12. Kuensel, 21-27 August 1999.
13. Times of India, New Delhi, 12 July 2013.
14. *Ibid.*, 23 July 2013.
15. Interview with Smita Gupta on 06 September, Times of India, New Delhi, 07 September 1994.
16. Kuensel, 26 August 1995.
17. *Ibid.*, 17 October 1998.
18. Bhutan in Focus, 2003, Royal Bhutanese Embassy, New Delhi, pp.19-20.
19. Leo E. Rose, n. 11, pp. 198-99.
20. *Ibid.*, p. 201.
21. *Ibid.*, pp.115-16.
22. Nari Rustomji, Bhutan: The Dragon Kingdom in Crisis, Oxford, 1978, p. 93.
23. Ram Rahul, Royal Bhutan, New Delhi,1983, p. 43.
24. Leo E. Rose, n. 11. p. 194.
25. Kuensel, 17-18 June 2010.
26. *Ibid.*, 16 September 1995.

11

Retrospect and Prospect

The factors which determine the foreign policy of a country are diverse—its geography, history, international setting, economic development, domestic milieu and the personality of the ruling elite. However, the geographical location of a country is a very critical factor in respect of its security. This is especially true in case of a small country like Bhutan. In the eighteenth century the country became sandwiched between two empires: the Manchu empire to the north and the East India Company to the south. Bhutan started facing aggressions from the both sides. The very survival of Bhutan as an independent country came under the threat. Hence Bhutan adopted isolationist policy to ward off its embroilment with its neighbours.

China which had been endeavouring to extend its suzerainty over Bhutan since it established its suzerainty over Tibet in the eighteenth century, intensified its efforts to attain its objective in the wake of the withdrawal of British troops from the Chumbi Valley in 1908. King Ugyen Wangchuck cast his lot with the British in India in order to survive as an independent ruler, and signed a treaty with the British in 1910, by which Bhutan agreed to be guided by the advice of the British Government of India in regard to its external relations and the British Government undertook to exercise no interference in the internal affairs of Bhutan. The treaty of 1910 proved an effective means to checkmate China's ambitions to establish its suzerainty over Bhutan. Moreover, Bhutan refrained itself from interacting with China in the light of Chinese aggressive activities.

Bhutan also began to face hostilities from its southern neighbour, viz., the East India Company which had established its rule in Bengal in the second half of the eighteenth century. In 1772, the Company intervened in the conflict between Bhutan and Cooch Behar, and launched hostilities against Bhutan, and captured Bhutanese territories. However, the Company made a gesture of goodwill towards the Deb Raja of Bhutan with a view to promoting its trade with the Himalayan countries, and returned the Bhutanese territories on the conclusion of war. After the agreement of peace and the restoration of the territories to Bhutan the Company authorities made repeated endeavours to establish commercial relations with Bhutan but they failed. As a matter of fact, the policy objectives of Bhutan were at odds with those of the Company. Bhutan was intent on maintaining its sovereignty: it was not prepared to surrender its people to the Company for the trial for any crime committed in the Company territory. The Bhutanese authorities also made efforts to keep the Company authorities at arm's length since the former feared that the latter would appropriate their territories. Hence the relations between Bhutan and the Company became strained by their disputes in respect of territory and the extradition of offenders. On 7 August 1837, the Company appointed Captain Pemberton to proceed on a mission to Bhutan to negotiate with the Deb Raja. Pemberton was directed to persuade the Government of Bhutan to transfer to the Company the possession of the Assam Dooars in lieu of the annual payment of a fixed sum. He was also asked to improve commercial relations with Bhutan. He reached Punakha on 02 April 1838. He drew up a treaty which stipulated, among other things, an unrestricted interactions between the people of Bhutan and the Company territory, and the extradition of offenders. On 25 April 1838, when the treaty was submitted to the Government of Bhutan, the Deb Raja refused to sign the treaty. The Bhutanese authorities feared that the ultimate object of the British mission was the conquest of Bhutan. Pemberton was not allowed to communicate with the Bhutanese people, and the movements of the members of his mission were closely watched by Bhutanese authorities. The Pemberton mission failed and withdrew from Bhutan on 09 May 1838.

After the failure of the Pemberton mission, the Company abandoned the policy of negotiation for the settlement of differences, and took recourse to coercive measures. The Assam Dooars were annexed in 1841. The Bhutanese authorities became incensed at the annexation of Assam Dooars by the Company. The relations between Bhutan and the Company deteriorated. In the 1850s, the march of events headed towards a confrontation which was, however, averted for the time being by the outbreak of revolt against the British in India in 1857. After the suppression of the revolt of 1857, the Government of British India turned its attention to its relations with Bhutan. It resorted to coercive measures, and in 1860, occupied Ambari Falakata, Bhutanese territory on the west of Teesta. However, it decided to resume the policy of negotiation, and in 1863, appointed Ashley Eden as its envoy to negotiate with the Government of Bhutan. Eden was directed to explain to the Government of Bhutan the reasons for withholding the revenue of Ambari Falakata by the British. He was instructed to arrange for free commerce between the people of the two countries. He was asked to demand the extradition of all captives detained in Bhutan. He was told that in respect of extradition of offenders, there could be no strict reciprocity between the two governments because of unequal levels of civilisation in Bhutan and British India. He was also directed to seek the appointment of an agent of the Government of British India in Bhutan.

Ashley Eden reached Punakha on 15 March 1864, and presented to the Government of Bhutan the draft treaty embodying the demands of the Government of British Indian Government. The Bhutanese authorities raised objections to the clauses of free commerce between the two countries and the appointment of an agent of British India at Punakha. They also said that a clause should be added to treaty restoring the Assam Dooars to Bhutan. On 24 March 1864, the Bhutanese authorities and Eden sat down to conclude their negotiations, and the Bhutanese authorities repeated their demand. When Eden refused to agree to their demand, he was publicly insulted and derided in the Bhutanese court. The alleged ill-treatment of Eden by the Bhutanese authorities became the main cause of the war which the Government of British India declared on 12 November 1864. The war between British India and Bhutan continued almost for a year. The Government of Bhutan had to sign a treaty at Sinchula on 11 November 1865, under which the Government of British India annexed the Bengal Dooars and the hilly tract on the left bank of the Teesta.

The Bhutanese authorities had been wary of the expansionist policy of the British in India since the East India Company established its authority in Bengal. The war and imposition of harsh terms of the Sinchula treaty had strong impact on the Bhutanese authorities. It hardened their resolve to insulate their country from all contacts with the outside world. Bhutan became virtually a forbidden land in the wake of the 1864-65 war.

Bhutan suffered foreign aggressions largely because of its small size. Small states were usually dominated by big Powers in the period prior to the Second World War. They could barely play any role in the international politics. The post-war period witnessed significant changes in the international politics. Many small States adopted active foreign policy through their membership of the UN and the Non-Aligned Movement.

Bhutan, however, continued to be concerned about its security and followed its isolationist policy for several years in the post-war period. One of the compelling reasons behind its decision was the continuance of the hostile environment in its northern neighbourhood. Soon after establishing its rule in China, the Communist regime under Mao Zedong sent its People's Liberation Army (PLA) into Tibet. The Chinese invasion on Tibet had strong repercussions in India and the Himalayan Kingdoms of Nepal and Bhutan. Hence China resorted to a stratagem to mollify them: it agreed that it would maintain the political autonomy and religious freedom of Tibet. But the Chinese Government started establishing its totalitarian regime in Tibet in the 1950s. Its hostility towards Bhutan also became obvious by 1959 when Chinese troops forcibly occupied Bhutanese enclaves in Tibet. The ruthless repression launched by the Chinese forces in Tibet forced the Dalai Lama to leave Tibet for India in 1959. Consequently, Bhutan snapped its ties with Tibet and sealed off its border with the latter.

Bhutan adopted a policy of caution and circumspection with China, and remained neutral in the boundary dispute between China and India. Nevertheless, the Chinese began intruding into the Bhutanese territory in the 1960s. It used to be in the form of Tibetan graziers intruding into the Bhutanese pasture-land. In the 1970s the Tibetan intrusions into the Bhutanese territory increased. Tibetan herdsmen intruded not only into the western sector of Bhutan but also into the central sector. In 1979, the Tibetan incursions into the Bhutanese territory took place on a large scale. This incident led Bhutan to decide on entering into direct negotiations with China on the delineation and demarcation of the boundary. The first boundary talks between Bhutan and China was held in Beijing in April 1984. In years between April 1984 and January 2010, 19 rounds of boundary talks took place between Bhutan and China, but the boundary dispute between the two countries could not be resolved. Bhutan has been eager that its traditional pasture-land on which its yak herders depended for their livelihood be restored to them. But China is bent on retaining the Bhutanese land because of its strategic importance. Possibly other country with China's size and resources could have acted magnanimously towards a small country like Bhutan. But Communist China has been following an expansionist policy towards its southern neighbouring country.

In contrast to its northern environment, Bhutan's southern environment was most friendly. While in the north the Communist regime led by Mao Zedong followed in the footsteps of expansionist Manchu emperors, and occupied Tibet in 1950, in the south Jawaharlal Nehru, the then leader of the Indian National Congress, declared on 7 September 1946, soon after assuming charge of foreign affairs in the interim Government of India, that India would develop close and friendly relations with other countries in the furtherance of world peace and freedom, and would not seek domination over other peoples. After the British formally transferred power to India on 15 August 1947, the Government of India led by Prime Minister Nehru decided on developing a new relationship with Bhutan, based on friendship and good neighbourliness. Hence on 08 August 1949, India and Bhutan concluded a new treaty to "promote and foster the relations of friendship and neighbourliness so necessary for the well-being of their peoples." Under the treaty India undertook to exercise no interference in the internal affairs of Bhutan while Bhutan agreed to be guided by the advice of the Government of India in regard to its external affairs. The treaty provided for free trade between India and Bhutan. India agreed to provide facilities for the carriage by land and water, of Bhutanese produce throughout its territory. The treaty gave Bhutan the right to import with the consent of India such arms, machinery and communication as might be needed for the security and welfare of Bhutan.

Moreover, India under Prime Minister Nehru made special efforts to strengthen friendly relations with Bhutan by returning to Bhutan about 32 square miles of territory in the Dewangiri district of Assam. Bhutan coveted this territory for a long time. In 1919, the Kingdom made a request to the Government of British India for the territory but the latter turned down the request on the ground that tea-gardens and plantations would be adversely affected by the advancement of the Bhutanese border. Prime Minister Nehru faced strong opposition to his move to transfer the territory to Bhutan. The opposition came not only from the Chief Minister of Assam but also from some members of the Indian Parliament. However, Prime Minister Nehru succeeded in overcoming the opposition, and transferred the territory to Bhutan.

The Kingdom of Bhutan responded to India's friendly gesture. King Jigme Dorji Wangchuck visited India and participated in India's Republic Day celebration on 26 January 1954. The King expressed his happiness at having come to India and establishing personal contacts with the Indian leaders. He invited Prime Minister Nehru to visit Bhutan. Prime Minister Nehru visited Bhutan in September 1958, and made it clear in a public meeting at Paro that India's only desire for Bhutan was that it should remain independent and choose its own direction and progress. Nehru also promised the economic and technical assistance that Bhutan needed for its economic development. But Bhutan was still disinclined to abandon its isolationist policy and accept Indian economic and technical aid. However, the hostile activities of Chinese troops in Tibet in 1959, had strong impact on the foreign policy of Bhutan. The ruthless suppression of popular uprisings in Tibet, which impelled the Dalai Lama to seek asylum in India had alarmed the Bhutanese ruling elite. They realised that the development of their country on modern lines was essential for its security and stability. Hence they eschewed their close-door policy and became earnest to develop their country with the Indian economic and technical assistance.

King Jigme Dorji Wangchuck opened up the Kingdom of Bhutan to the outside world. Bhutan joined the Colombo Plan in 1962, became member of the Universal Postal Union in 1969, and the United Nations in 1971. One of the reasons how Bhutan could change its foreign policy without any hindrance was that the country enjoyed the political stability under the monarchy. The King established the Bhutan-India friendship on a firm ground. Although the two countries had long political relations, there was little contact between two peoples. In the 1960s, Bhutan and India started an exchange of goodwill visits. King Jigme Dorji Wangchuck visited India in February 1961 and in April 1966. A seven-member delegation of the Royal Advisory Council of Bhutan paid a goodwill visit to India in December 1967. Morarji Desai, the then Deputy Prime Minister of India, paid a goodwill visit to Bhutan in March 1968. Indira Gandhi, the then Prime Minister of India, visited Bhutan in May 1968. Moreover, Bhutan and India appointed their diplomatic representatives for the first time in 1971. Bhutan appointed Pema Wangchuck as its first representative in New Delhi on 17 May 1971. India also appointed B. S. Das as its representative in Thimphu on 15 July 1971. The establishment of Bhutanese Embassy in India and Indian Embassy in Bhutan enhanced interactions between the people of the two countries.

King Jigme Singye Wangchuck, fourth king, who succeeded his father in 1972, played a very important role in strengthening friendship with India. He paid regular visits to New Delhi and met prominent Indian leaders. His visits contributed to consolidating Bhutan's friendship with India. In July 2006, when King Jigme Singye Wangchuck visited New Delhi, he requested the Government of India to update the Friendship Treaty, which was signed between Bhutan and India as early as on 8 August 1949, was out of tune with the changed national and international settings of both the countries. The updated Treaty of Friendship between Bhutan and India was signed in New Delhi on

08 February 2007. The signing of the updated treaty further strengthened Bhutan's friendship with India. After King Jigme Singye Wangchuck abdicated, his son and successor, Jigme Khesar Namgyel Wangchuck acceded to the Bhutanese throne in 2006. Since then Bhutan's friendship with India has deepened.

Bhutan also took steps to strengthen its relations with other South Asian countries besides India. It sought to establish friendly relations with Bangladesh because of its geographical proximity. The friendly feelings between the two peoples were established during the Bangladesh liberation war when Bhutan extended its sympathy and support to the people of Bangladesh. However, King Jigme Dorji Wangchuck foresaw in the emergence of Bangladesh as an independent country positive advantages for his country in the South Asian region. When Bangladesh became independent in December 1971, Bhutan was the second country after India to extend recognition to Bangladesh and establish diplomatic relations with that country. In April 1972, Dawa Tsering, the then Foreign Minister of Bhutan, visited Bangladesh and expressed Bhutan's desire to develop political and commercial relations with the new country of the region. Moreover, King Jigme Singye Wangchuck paid a state visit to Bangladesh in December 1974. The visit resulted in strengthening Bhutan's friendly relations and cooperation with Bangladesh.

In September 1980, Bhutan and Bangladesh signed an agreement trade. In accordance with the agreement the two countries accorded to each other the most favoured nation (MFN) treatment in respect of trade. They also undertook to provide means of transportation and warehousing to facilitate the movement of goods. However, the trade between Bhutan and Bangladesh had been very slow in picking up. In 1986, the Government of Bangladesh waived 50 per cent of tariff on imports from Bhutan. As a result, Bhutan began to have a favourable trade balance with Bangladesh. By 1989, Bhutan's trade surplus rose to about Nu 126.2 million. In recent years, Bhutan and Bangladesh both are making efforts to have a trade balance between their countries.

Bhutan also endeavoured to strengthen its relations with Nepal with which it had age-old ties. The relations between the two countries grew largely in religious and cultural fields. Bhutan was given control over Swambhunath and other Buddhist shrines in Nepal when Shabdrung Ngawang Namgyal was ruling over Bhutan. Moreover, Newar artisans and craftsmen visited Bhutan during this period. It was these artisans who decorated beautifully several monasteries including the Tago Monastery in Bhutan. But the relations between the two countries were adversely affected during the 1854-56 Nepal-Tibet war. The Buddhist shrines in Nepal were taken over by the Government of Nepal because Kathmandu suspected that Bhutan had aided the Tibetans during the war. However, the relations between the two countries remained peaceful and normal and the Bhutanese people continued to go to Nepal annually for pilgrimage. Since Bhutan follow an isolationist policy, its political relations with Nepal were limited. After Bhutan gave up its isolationist policy, its friendly relations with Nepal were restored. In 1969, Prince Namgyal Wangchuck visited Nepal and represented the King of Bhutan during the wedding ceremony of King Birendra.

The formal diplomatic relation between Bhutan and Nepal was established in 1983. The interactions between the two countries increased. The Bhutan-Nepal Friendship Association was established in November 1989. But Bhutan-Nepal friendship received a setback in 1990, when the Nepali Bhutanese especially the Nepali immigrants in Bhutan rose against the Bhutanese Government. When the Bhutanese authorities cracked down on the insurgents, a large number of Nepali Bhutanese fled Bhutan and went to eastern Nepal where they stayed in several camps. The exodus of Nepali Bhutanese to Nepal became a knotty issue between Bhutan and Nepal. While the Government of Nepal said that all those refugees who stayed in the camps in eastern Nepal were Bhutanese citizens and should return to Bhutan, but the Government of Bhutan did not accept the plea of the Government of Nepal. By 2003, Bhutan and Nepal had about 15 rounds of bilateral talks on the refugees staying in the camps in eastern Nepal. However, the talks between the two governments were stalled after the Bhutanese members of the Joint Verification Team (JVT) were attacked and injured in Jhapa on 22 December 2003. In 2008, when Prime Minster Jigmi Y. Thinley met Prime Minister Pushpa Kamal Dahal (Prachanda) of Nepal on the sidelines of the 63rd session of the UN General Assembly, they agreed to give a fresh look to their relations. They further agreed that the diversification of their relations should not be held ransom by the single issue of refugees in the camps.

Bhutan not only endeavoured to strengthen relations with its South Asian neighbours but also interested itself in the development of the South Asian Association of Regional Cooperation (SAARC). It has been an ardent supporter of the SAARC since its inception. It associated itself in the SAARC's integrated programme of action especially in the field of health (fight against leprosy), agriculture (potato cultivation) and postal services.

South Asian regional cooperation assumed a new dimension in Bhutan's foreign policy. Bhutan hosted the third ministerial meeting of South Asian Regional Cooperation on 13 May 1985. In his inaugural address, King Jigme Singye Wangchuck stressed the need of cooperation among the South Asian countries in the best interests of their people and the region. He said that it was essential for the countries of the region to improve their relations. He referred to the sentiment of nationalism which had given to each of South Asian countries such a strong sense of nationhood, pride and self-respect that had sometimes created hurdles in the development of mutual cooperation among them.

King Jigme Singye Wangchuck regarded mutual fears and apprehensions between South Asian countries as principal obstacles to regional cooperation. He, therefore, emphasised the need for a political understanding among South Asian countries to achieve a meaningful breakthrough in the SAARC. At the Dhaka Summit he said that it would be unrealistic to ignore the primacy of the political factor in the matter of regional cooperation. The King wanted to strengthen the popular base of the SAARC. Speaking at the SAARC Summit in Bangalore on 16 November 1986, the King called upon the ruling elite of the South Asian States to inculcate in the minds of the people of the region a sense of regional consciousness and to encourage people-to-people contacts in order to bring about a greater awareness of each other, and to generate a spirit of friendship and understanding in the region. King Jigme Singye Wangchuck held that the political milieu could be improved through the instrumentality of the SAARC. He said that the SAARC could play a decisive role in fostering better understanding among the South Asian countries and creating an atmosphere conducive to the promotion of peace and harmony in the region.

Bhutan's policy towards the SAARC was largely influenced by its desire to promote its political and economic interests. It sought to advance its political interest by strengthening its relations with the South Asian states. Since the SAARC was formed, it consolidated its relations with Bangladesh and India, and established diplomatic relations with Sri Lanka and Pakistan. Moreover, Bhutan wanted to strengthen the SAARC so that it could get economic and technical aid through the SAARC. Although it has been a developing country like other South Asian countries, it lagged much in developing its economy. It was only in 1961 that it embarked upon its economic development. Moreover, it lacked adequate economic resources. Hence Bhutan emphasised the need for mobilising economic resources on the regional level. Addressing the sixth SAARC Summit in Colombo in December 1991, King Jigme Singye Wangchuck said that he regarded the lack of fund as one of the biggest obstacles to developing the economy of South Asian countries, and proposed the establishment of a SAARC Development Fund, which would provide finance for industrial development, poverty alleviation, protection of environment, and balance of payment support for the countries in the South Asian region. The Heads of member-countries of the SAARC approved the proposal for the SAARC Development Fund during the SAARC Summit held in Colombo on 02-03 August 2008.

Moreover, Bhutan hosted the SAARC Summit for the first time in Thimphu in April 2010. The Thimphu Summit issued a joint declaration on climate change to address the adverse effects of climate change in the region. One of the significant achievements of this Summit was operationalisation of the South Asian University in New Delhi. The University has become the centre of excellence for higher education in South Asia. Moreover, the hosting of the SAARC Summit in Thimphu was a master-stroke of Bhutan's foreign policy. It raised Bhutan's standing in the comity of South Asian nations.

Bhutan has continued to highlight the unfinished agenda of the regional cooperation. At the SAARC Summit held in Kathmandu on 26 November 2014, it stressed the need to tackle cross-border crimes like terrorism, trafficking in human beings and drugs, as well as to address challenges like climate change and poverty alleviation.

In 2004, Bhutan also joined the Bay of Bengal Initiative for Multi-Sectoral Technical and Economic Cooperation (BIMSTEC), another regional organisation, which was set up in 1997 and whose main purpose is to serve as a link between South Asia and South East Asia for better trade, transport and overall development in the region. Bhutan's membership of the

BIMSTEC was a step towards its goal of integrating itself with the regional and global markets.

Jigmi Y. Thinley, the then Prime Minister of Bhutan, participated in the BIMSTEC Summit held in New Delhi on 13 November 2008. Prime Minister Thinley supported the initiative to make the BIMSTEC area a free trade zone. He said that the escalating price of energy was a problem and that BIMSTEC would have to intensify cooperation and make use of energy resources available in the region. He called for promoting greater intra-BIMSTEC tourism using the region's rich and diverse culture and history. The Prime Minister of Bhutan welcomed the BIMSTEC Convention on international terrorism, crime and drug trafficking. He also asked the member-countries of the BIMSTEC to set up practical mechanism at the earliest for the effective implementation of the Convention.

Bhutan participated not only in the subordinate state system of South Asia and South East Asia but also in the global system. Since 1971, when it became a member of the UN, it formulated its global policy. Although Bhutan's global policy has been, to all intents and purposes, similar to that of other developing countries, it has been concerned more about the need of peace in the world and the importance of the UN's role in this respect inasmuch as its weltanschauung has been influenced by its Buddhist religion and culture. It committed itself to the ideals of the UN Charter and its purposes. In the UN, Bhutan emphasised the importance of peace and stressed the need of disarmament for maintenance of peace in the world. Bhutan opposed colonialism, imperialism and racism, which, it said, constituted a grave threat to international peace and security. Bhutan assailed power politics among nations and pointed out that such a policy only created the competitive arms race between countries, and increased threats to international peace and security. Bhutan strongly supported efforts to establish New International

Economic Order, and pleaded for economic aid for developing countries especially landlocked and least developed countries.

Bhutan expressed its desire to ensure that the Indian Ocean and its adjoining areas should be free from becoming an area of confrontation between big powers. It supported the proposal to declare the Indian Ocean as a zone of peace. Bhutan also held that UN needed a degree of reform in order to face new challenges of the twenty first century. It believed that the Security Council should be expanded to allow greater representation to developing countries. In this context, Bhutan strongly supported India's candidature for a permanent seat on the Security Council.

Bhutan adopted the policy of non-alignment, and became a member of the non-aligned group in 1973. It emphasised the importance of non-aligned movement for maintaining peace in the world. It said that the main objective of the non-aligned movement was to be achievement of peace based on the application of the principles of peaceful co-existence, national independence, sovereign equality, non-interference in the internal affairs of states and the right of peoples to self-determination. According to Bhutan, the non-aligned movement was averse to all forms of subjugations, dependence, interference and intervention. Bhutan assailed armed interventions in South-West and South-East Asia in 1979. It supported the struggle of the Palestinian people for their right to self-determination in their homeland. It condemned the brutal system of apartheid in South Africa.

Bhutan stressed the need of disarmament in the non-aligned conferences. It deplored that several countries continued to spend huge amounts on armament as compared to what was spent on human development. It said that as a Buddhist State deeply imbued with the values of non-violence and brotherhood, it was resolutely averse to armament and armed struggle. Bhutan emphasised the need to bring about general and complete disarmament, particularly nuclear disarmament. Bhutan also dwelt on the economic dimension of the non-aligned movement. It highlighted deteriorating economic conditions of developing countries especially landlocked and least developed countries. It pleaded for economic aid for these countries. Bhutan attached great importance to economic cooperation among developing countries. It urged the member-countries of non-aligned movement to take measures to make South-South Cooperation meaningful and effective. It also asked them to enhance its efforts to renew the North-South dialogue with a view to achieving its goal of establishing a New International Economic Order.

Bhutan used the tools of foreign policy and diplomacy to propagate its unique cultural identity in foreign countries. In 1989, Bhutan's Special Commission for Cultural Affairs organised cultural exhibitions in the United States and Japan. The one-year exhibition with its theme "Spiritual Arts of Bhutan" was aimed at creating wider understanding and appreciation among the Americans and the Japanese of its distinctive aspects of the rich and ancient culture. Although Bhutan had not established diplomatic relations with the USA, it developed ties with the USA in cultural and educational fields. There have been exchanges of visits of officials and academics between the two countries. Bhutan also organised cultural exhibitions in several European countries. In 1998-99, it organised exhibitions in Austria, Switzerland and Spain. The Bhutan exhibition was an elaborate depiction of Bhutan's religious and cultural antiques, which included the Raven Crown of King Jigme Namgay, a sword of the third King, Jigme Dorji Wangchuck, a carving of Milla Repa and Marpa on the horn of rhinoceros and numerous ancient statues.

Bhutan's cultural diplomacy and its foreign policy statements in the UN General Assembly, meetings of non-aligned countries, and in ESCAP, UNCTAD, and Group of 77 meetings proved fruitful. The international community started providing development assistance to Bhutan. Initially foreign aid came only from India. But Bhutan began to get aid from third countries from its Fourth Five Year Plan (1976-81). It received development aid from such countries as Australia, Austria, Canada, Japan, New Zealand, The Netherland, and Switzerland.

Bhutan also obtained aid from several multilateral organisations. It joined the UN in 1971, and started receiving aid from UN agencies like the UNDP and the UNCDF from its Third Plan (1971-76) onwards. It joined the World Bank and the Asian Development Bank in 1981, and received aid from those institutions for Fifth Plan (1981-87) and thereafter. The multilateral aid to Bhutan has been quite substantial. By 2014, aid received from the International Development Association (IDA) was about $253861776. 14.

However, India remains the largest source of aid. Since 1961, when Bhutan embarked on its First Five Year Plan, India continued to be the major donor for Bhutan's economic development. Ten Five Year Plans have been completed, the first two entirely financed by India. Some of the major development projects in Bhutan implemented with Indian assistance are a network of roads, Paro Airport, Bhutan Broadcasting Station, several schools and hospitals. By 2007, India invested about Rs 5000 crore in the construction of three hydropower projects—Chukkha, Kurichu and Tala. These have a combined installed capacity of about 1400 MW which supply India with power and have become in the process symbols of Bhutan-India friendship and partnership for mutual benefit. India's assistance to Bhutan's Tenth Five Year Plan (July 2008—June 2013) was Rs 34 billion. Moreover, in 2010, India has agreed to assist Bhutan in building the Punatsangchhu-11 (1000 MW), Mangdechhu (720 MW) and Sankosh (4060 MW) at the estimated cost of Rs 500 billion on the basis of 70 per cent loan and 30 per cent grant. Thus, the Bhutanese ruling elite endeavoured to develop their country with the help of bilateral and multilateral development aid.

Moreover, Bhutan raised its stock in the comity of nations by following peaceful and friendly policy not only with its South Asian neighbours but also with most countries of the world. In making of Bhutan's foreign policy the Bhutanese political institutions such as the monarchy, the National Assembly, the Royal Advisory Council, the Ministry of Foreign Affairs the Royal Bhutan Army, Civil Servant and pressure groups have played an important role.

The Bhutanese rulers during the Shabdrung period adopted isolationist policy when their country's security was threatened by foreign imperialists from northern and southern directions. However, it was the monarchy which strengthened this policy. King Ugyen Wangchuck and King Jigme Wangchuck virtually stopped interactions with their neighbours. They prevented the entry of foreigners in their country, and refused to appoint representatives of foreign countries in their Kingdom.

Initially King Jigme Dorji Wangchuck, third king, also followed isolationist policy. In 1958, when Prime Minister Nehru visited Bhutan and offered economic and technical assistance, the King did not accept Indian assistance. However, King Jigme Dorji Wangchuck was impelled to change his country's foreign policy in the light of what happened in Tibet in 1959. In 1960-61, the King embarked upon developing the economy of Bhutan with India's financial and technical assistance. He opened up his Kingdom to the world. Bhutan joined the Colombo Plan (1962), the Universal Postal Union (1969), and the UN (1971).

King Jigme Singye Wangchuck, fourth King, played a significant role in formulating Bhutan's foreign policy. He visited New Delhi several occasions and strengthened Bhutan's relations with India. The King addressed several SAARC Summits and Non-aligned Summits, and raised the Kingdom's standing in the comity of nations. King Jigme Khesar Namgyel Wangchuck, the present King, who became the fifth King of Bhutan in 2006, follows in his father's footsteps in the sphere of his country's foreign policy. He visited India several times and strengthened relations with India. Moreover, the King has been following the policy of peace and friendship with all countries of the world.

The Bhutanese Agents in India acted as advisors to the Kings of Bhutan, and played important roles in making of Bhutan's foreign policy. Ugyen Dorji who had free access to the Tibetan authorities, was appointed Agent of Bhutan at Kalimpong in 1889. He brought about close understandings between the Bhutanese authorities and the British in India. Ugyen Dorji played a significant role in negotiating the Treaty of 1910 between Bhutan and British India. His son and successor, Sonam T. Dorji advised King Jigme Wangchuck, Bhutan's second king, to maintain friendly relations with British India.

Among the Bhutanese Prime Ministers who played a significant role in formulating Bhutan's foreign policy was Prime Minister Jigmie Dorji. He advised King Jigme Dorji Wangchuck to establish close relations with India inasmuch as he saw the Kingdom's security threatened by China. Jigmi Y. Thinley who became the first democratically elected Prime Minister of Bhutan in 2008, sought to spread in foreign countries Bhutan's development philosophy: gross happiness of the people is better than gross domestic product, proclaimed by King Jigme Singye Wangchuck. He also expanded Bhutan's diplomatic ties from 21 to 53 countries between 2008 and 2013. Tshering Tobgay, who became Prime Minister of Bhutan in 2013, made it clear that he was fully aware of his country's geographical realities. Prime Minister Tobgay follows policy of peace and friendship in the region and the world.

Among the Foreign Ministers who played important role in making of Bhutan's foreign policy the name of Dawa Tsering stands out. He was appointed Minister of Foreign Affairs of Bhutan in 1972, and remained at that post till 1998. He led Bhutanese delegations to several UN and non-aligned meetings. He took steps to strengthen Bhutan-India relations. He also took initiatives in starting talks on the Bhutan-China boundary dispute.

In 1998, Jigmi Y. Thinley became Foreign Minister of Bhutan. He also played an important role in formulating the foreign policy of Bhutan. He addressed the 53rd session of the UN General Assembly. He pleaded not only for complete disarmament but also for inclusion of India and Japan as permanent members of the Security Council. He signed an agreement with China in 1998, on maintaining status quo on Bhutan-China border. Khandu Wangchuck who became Bhutan's Foreign Minister followed by and large in the footsteps of his predecessors in the sphere of the country's foreign policy. He addressed the 58th session of the UN General Assembly, and stressed the need of peace and security in the world.

The National Assembly of Bhutan also played a role in making of the Kingdom's foreign policy. The members of the National Assembly often raised and discussed the foreign policy issues of Bhutan. In May 1960, they raised the issue of Bhutan-India boundary as shown in maps published by the Government of India in its White Paper on its relations with China. Bhutan-India boundary had been shown in maps by a thin line as that separating Indian states. The members of the National Assembly demanded that the boundary line should be marked thicker and in deeper colour so as to look like an international boundary. They also expressed their concern over Bhutan-China boundary dispute. They said that if Bhutan's traditional boundary was altered in favour of China, it would adversely affect the economy of Bhutanese yak herders. They requested the Government of Bhutan to ensure that Bhutan's traditional boundary be maintained.

In several developing countries the army and civil servants play an important role in making of foreign policy. In Bhutan, there was no standing army until the mid-1950s. King Jigme Dorji Wangchuck took steps to organise the Royal Bhutan Army (RBA). By 1964, the size of the RBA rose to 9,000 strong. A section of the Bhutanese army, especially those belonging to the traditional group deprecated the Bhutanese Government's policy of modernising the country with foreign assistance. This resulted into the assassination of Prime Minister Jigmie Dorji on 05 April 1964. However, there was no attempt by army at seizing the political power of the Kingdom. The King who was in Switzerland for medical treatment, returned and resumed control over the army. Since 1964, the Royal Bhutan Army has been completely loyal to the civilian authority of the Kingdom.

The civil servants especially those belonging to the ministry of foreign affairs play an important role in making of foreign policy of their countries. In Bhutan there was no civil service in terms of modern concept prior to the 1960s. During the reign of the first two kings the number of officials was very small, who administered the country from a room in the Royal Palace at Bumthang. When King Jigme Dorji Wangchuck embarked upon the kingdom's economic development, it became essential to create an efficient civil service. In 1960, a new administrative structure was constructed at Tashichhodzong in Thimphu. With the creation of a council of ministers, the number of civil servants increased. In Bhutan, civil servants played an important role in formulating the foreign policy of their country. Prior to 2008, some of the civil servants rose to the post of foreign minister in Bhutan.

Bhutan would continue to pursue the policy of peace and friendship with its neighbours. However, its policy towards China largely depends on the Chinese attitude. Bhutan has not been able to establish its diplomatic relations with China because of the latter's imperialist and expansionist policy. If China had recognised Bhutan's traditional boundary with Tibet, Bhutan would have normalised its relations with China. Moreover, if China had restored Tibet's autonomy, Bhutan's traditional relationship with Tibet would have been resumed. One could hope there would be a change for better in the Chinese attitude.

Bhutan would continue to strengthen its friendly relationship with India. It is not only geographical proximity that binds the two countries together but there are political, economic and cultural factors which impel them to come closer. Unlike China's repressive political system which seems to be an anathema to the Bhutanese people, there is no antipathy between the Bhutanese constitutional monarchy and Indian democracy. Moreover, the cultural affinity between the Bhutanese and the Indian people brings them together. Furthermore, the relations between Bhutan and India have been strengthened by economic underpinnings. Bhutan has developed most of its industries and hydropower projects with India's financial assistance in its southern region which is contiguous with India. Bhutan and India both are beneficiaries of economic partnership.

The foreign policy of a country is interrelated with its domestic politics. If a country is embroiled in its domestic crisis, it would not be able to formulate a sound and successful foreign policy. The King of Bhutan has been successful in maintaining political stability in his kingdom. Some scholars hold that the country which is under the monarchy is prone to political turmoil. Samuel P. Huntington in his book, *Political Order in Changing Societies* (New Haven, 1970) projected a bleak future for modernising monarchies. According to Huntington, the centralisation of power is necessary to promote social and economic reforms but the new groups produced by the reforms would not be assimilated into the political system and would rise against the monarchy. However, the Bhutanese ruling elite have been sagacious and foresighted. They have followed the path of decentralisation and democratisation rather than centralisation of power. King Jigme Singye Wangchuck took steps in decentralising the administration and involving the Bhutanese people in the decision-making process. He established the District Development Committee in every district between 1976 and 1981. In 1991, the King also established the Block Development Committees in every block to promote further decentralisation. Moreover, in 2008, Bhutan adopted a constitution by which the country has become a democratic constitutional monarchy. The executive power of the State has been vested in the cabinet headed by Prime Minister of Bhutan. Besides, Bhutan has taken steps to forestall political problems in the country. Under the Constitution political leaders are forbidden from resorting to regionalism, ethnicity and religion to incite voters for electoral gain. Moreover, unlike other countries there is no probability of a hung parliament in Bhutan. Under the Constitution only two political parties which have the highest number of votes in the primary election could contest in the general election. The party which would win the majority of seats in the National Assembly would be the ruling party and the other party would be the opposition party. Thus, there is no threat to political stability in the kingdom. Bhutan would continue to pursue policy of peace and friendship in the region and the world.

Appendices

Appendix 1

Letter from the Government of India to the Secretary of State for India, dated 1st October 1908, concerning Chinese activity on the North-Eastern Frontier and the relations of the Government of India with Bhutan.

For some months past our attention has been called to the unusual energy of the Chinese in Tibet and their obvious preparations for an active policy on our North-Eastern Frontier.

Apart from any question of new movements in China, the action of the Chinese in Tibet clearly proves their purpose to establish effective dominion in that country. The transfer of Chao ErhFeng, the able and determined Viceroy of Szechuan, to Lhasa; the assignment on Szechuan revenue of a grant of 400,000 to 500,000 taels per annum for the reorganisation of the Tibetan administration; the appointment of Chao ErhFeng's brother to the Szechuan Viceroyalty with a view to avoiding friction and ensuring harmonious cooperation, the occupation by Chinese troops of Chamdo and other portions of Eastern Tibet; the establishment of a military post at Nagchuka north of Lhasa; the increase of the Lhasa garrison to 1,500 Chinese and 3,000 Tibetan troops; the efforts to raise a Tibetan army stiffened by Chinese troops, and the proclamation issued in this connection; all this evidence, which has been collected from the reports of our local officers, the specially valuable letters of the Nepalese representatives in Tibet, and the despatches of His Majesty's Minister at Peking, points unmistakably to the existence and steady accomplishment of a clearly defined policy.

It is early as yet to forecast the future relations in Tibet of the Chinese and Tibetans to one another and to ourselves; but it is clear that the status quo on this part of the frontier has already been materially altered. The policy which H.M.'s Government have laid down in regard to Tibet limits our interest in purely Tibetan affairs to the observance of treaties and trade regulations. The local Chinese and Tibetan officials are still obstructive, and the appointment of Chang Tachen to the Wai-wu-pu does not augur well for conciliation and accommodation in the near future. Our officials, however, must keep on the best terms possible with both Chinese and Tibetans, not yielding our rights under treaty or agreement, but not seeking to push forward our interests. In other words, we must pursue a policy of watchful inactivity.

The portion of Tibet bordering on India is cold and infertile, incapable of supporting any considerable number of troops. The states intervening between Tibet and the plains of India are, on the other hand, temperate and fertile countries capable now, or in the near future, of supporting troops in large numbers. Nepal already supports an army, and the virgin soil of Sikkim and Bhutan is fast being brought under cultivation. The Chinese evidently realise the importance of obtaining a footing in these countries. When in a figure of speech, Chang Tachen likened the union of China, Tibet, Nepal, Sikkim and Bhutan to the blending of the five colours, and compared the position of Tibet, Nepal, Sikkim and Bhutan to that of molar teeth side by side in a man's mouth, he doubtless gave expression to Chinese aspirations. From his position in the Wai-wu-pu, Chang Tachen will be able to promote those aspirations, which, indeed have already taken shape in a deliberate attempt to obtain some recognition by Bhutan of the suzerainty of China.

At the beginning of April, Ma Chi Fu, late Popon of the Chumbi Valley, set out for Bhutan with a guard of twenty Chinese soldiers and attended by the Tibetan physician to the Phari Jongpens. A few days later the Bhutan Agent, Ugyen Kazi, showed Mr Bell copies of two letters which the Maharaja of Bhutan had received from the Amban at Lhasa and the Popon of Pipitang in the Chumbi Valley. The Amban's letter, after reciting that Bhutan was under the suzerainty of China and was the southern gate of the Chinese Empire, informed the Maharaja that he was sending an officer to report on the condition of the country. The Popon's letter, which was very peremptorily worded, ordered the attendance of the Ponlops and barons at the boundaries of their fiefs to conduct the Chinese mission through them. Mr Bell assures us that there can be no doubt as to the genuineness of these letters; although not allowed to take copies of them he was able to examine them carefully. He was also permitted to see the correspondences which have passed between the Maharaja and his Agent on the subject. The Maharaja wrote that, since the establishment of the present regime in Bhutan, some 240 years ago, there had been no record of any Chinese mission coming to Bhutan or of China claiming suzerainty over it. The Agent advised the Maharaja to reply that when engaged in war against the British, Bhutan had received no assistance from China, that she had never paid tribute to China, nor had any of her officials been paid by China. In the result, Ma Chi Fu received so unmistakable a rebuff that he proceeded no further than Paro and returned to Tibet early in May.

Thus, the attempted assertion of suzerainty over Bhutan failed; but there is every likelihood that it will be renewed. And assuredly it will be renewed with greater insistence as the Chinese strengthen their hold on the Chumbi Valley. Now we cannot afford to let the Chinese establish influence in Bhutan. We are strongly of opinion that the time has come to frustrate the evident designs of China on Bhutan; and local conditions are favourable for a blocking policy. The Maharaja of Bhutan is well disposed towards us and is highly incensed with the Chinese and Tibetans over a fracas which took place quite recently between some Bhutanese and the Chinese and Tibetans at Phari.

We, therefore, recommend to your Lordship that Mr Bell should proceed quietly to Bhutan at an early date and enter into negotiations with the Maharaja. We enclose a draft treaty to form the basis of discussion between Mr Bell and the Maharaja. It may be necessary to guarantee the Maharaja against aggression, and we suggest that Mr Bell should be authorised to incorporate some provision to this end in the treaty, should the Maharaja insist upon it.

Appendix 2

Treaty of Punakha, 1910

Treaty between His Excellency Earl of Minto, Viceroy and Governor-General of India in Council, and His Highness Ugyen Wangchuck, Maharaja of Bhutan.

"The British Government undertakes to exercise no interference in the internal administration of Bhutan. On its part, the Bhutanese Government agrees to be guided by the advice of the British Government in regard to its external relations. In the event of disputes with or causes of complaint against the Maharajas of Sikkim and Cooch Behar, such matters will be referred for arbitration to the British Government which will settle them in such manner as justice may require, and insist upon the observance of its decisions by the Maharajas named."

Done in quadruplicate at Punakha, Bhutan, this eightieth day of January in the year of our Lord one thousand nine hundred and ten, corresponding with the Bhutea date, the 27th day of the 11th month of the Earth-Bird (Sa-ja) year.

Appendix 3

Indo-Bhutanese Friendship Treaty, 1949

The Government of India on the one part, and His Highness the Druk Gyalpo's Government on the other part, equally animated by the desire to regulate in a friendly manner and upon a solid and durable basis the state of affairs caused by the termination of the British Government's authority in India, and to promote and foster the relations of friendship and neighbourliness so necessary for the wellbeing of their peoples, have resolved to conclude the following treaty, and have, for this purpose named their representatives, that is to say, Sir Harishwar Dayal representing the Government of India, who has full powers to agree to the said treaty on behalf of the Government of India, and Deb Zimpon Sonam Tobgay Dorji, Yang-Lop Sonam, Chho-Zim Thondup,Rin-Zim Tandin and Ha Drung Jigmie Palden Dorji, representing the Government of His Highness the Druk Gyalpo, Maharaja of Bhutan, who have full powers to agree to the same on behalf of the Government of Bhutan.

Article 1

There shall be perpetual peace and friendship between the Government of India and the Government of Bhutan.

Article 2

The Government of India undertakes to exercise no interference in the internal administration of Bhutan. On its part the Government of

Bhutan agrees to be guided by the advice of the Government of India in regard to its external relations.

Article 3

In place of the compensation granted to the Government of Bhutan under Article 4 of the Treaty of Sinchula and enhanced by the treaty of the eighth day of January 1910 and the temporary subsidy of Rupees one lakh per annum granted in 1942, the Government of India agrees to make an annual payment of Rupees five lakhs to the Government of Bhutan. And it is further hereby ageed that the said annual payment shall be made on the tenth day of January every year, the first payment being made on the tenth day of January 1950. This payment shall continue as long as this treaty remains in force and its terms are duly observed.

Article 4

Further to mark the friendship existing and continuing between the said Governments, the Government of India shall within one year from the date of signature of this treaty, return to the Government of Bhutan about thirty-two square miles of territory in the area known as Dewangiri. The Government of India shall appoint a competent officer or officers to mark out the area so returned to the Government of Bhutan.

Article 5

There shall, as heretofore, be free trade and commerce between the territories of the Government of India and of the Government of Bhutan; the Government of India agrees to grant the Government of Bhutan every facility for the carriage, by land and water, of its produce throughout the territory of the Government of India, including the right to use such forest roads as may be specified by mutual agreement from time to time.

Article 6

The Government of India agrees that the Government of Bhutan shall be free to import with the assistance and approval of the Government of India, from or through India into Bhutan, whatever arms, ammunition, machinery, warlike material or stores may be required or desired for the strength and welfare of Bhutan, and that this arrangement shall hold good for all time as long as the Government of India is satisfied that the intentions of the Government of Bhutan are friendly and that there is no danger to India from such importations. The Government of Bhutan, on other hand, agrees that there shall be no export of such arms, ammunition, etc. across the frontier of Bhutan either by the Government of Bhutan or by private individuals.

Article 7

The Government of India and the Government of Bhutan agree that Bhutanese subjects residing in Indian territories shall have equal justice with Indian subjects, and that Indian subjects residing in Bhutan shall have equal justice with the subjects of the Government of Bhutan.

Article 8

(1) The Government of India shall, on demand being duly made in writing by the Government of Bhutan, take proceedings in accordance with the provisions of the Indian Extradition Act, 1903 (of which a copy shall be furnished to the Government of Bhutan), for the surrender of all Bhutanese subjects accused of any crimes specified in the first schedule of the said Act who may take refuge in Indian territory.

(2) The Government of Bhutan shall, on requisition being made by the Government of India, or by any officer authorised by the Government of India in this behalf, surrender any Indian subjects, or subjects of a foreign power, whose extradition may be required in pursuance of any agreement or arrangements made by the Government of India with the said power, accused of any of the crimes, specified in the first schedule of Act XV of 1903, who may take refuge in the territory under the jurisdiction of the Government of Bhutan, and also any Bhutanese subjects who, after committing any of the crimes referred to in Indian territory, shall flee into Bhutan, on such evidence of their guilt being produced as shall satisfy the local court of the district in which the offence may have been committed.

Article 9

Any differences and disputes arising in the application or interpretation of this treaty shall in the first instance be settled by negotiation. If within three months of the start of negotiations no settlement is arrived at, then the matter shall be referred to the arbitration of three arbitrators, who shall be nationals of either India or Bhutan, chosen in the following manner:

(1) One person nominated by the Government of India;
(2) One person nominated by the Government of Bhutan;
(3) A judge of the Federal Court, or of a High Court in India, to be chosen by the Government of Bhutan, who shall be Chairman.

The judgment of this Tribunal shall be final and executed without delay by either party.

Article 10

This treaty shall continue in force in perpetuity unless terminated or modified by mutual consent.

Done in duplicate at Darjeeling this eighth day of August, One thousand nine hundred and fortynine, corresponding with the Bhutanese date the fifteenth day of the sixth month of the Earth-Bull year.

Appendix 4

Treaty of Friendship between the Government of the Republic of India and the Royal Government of Bhutan, New Delhi, 08 February 2007.

The Government of the Republic of India and the Government of Bhutan:

Reaffirming their respect for each other's independence, sovereignty and territorial integrity;

Recalling the historical relations that have existed between our two countries;

Recognising with deep satisfaction the manner in which these relations have evolved and matured over the years into model of good neighbourly relations;

Being fully committed to further strengthening this enduring and mutually beneficial relationship based on genuine goodwill and friendship, shared interests, and close understanding and cooperation;

Desiring to clearly reflect this exemplary relationship as it stands today;

And having decided, through mutual consent, to update the 1949 Treaty relating to the promotion of, and fostering the relations of friendship and neighbourliness between India and Bhutan;

Have agreed as follows:

Article 1

There shall be perpetual peace and friendship between India and Bhutan.

Article 2

In keeping with the abiding ties of close friendship and cooperation between Bhutan and India, the Government of the kingdom of Bhutan and the Government of the Republic of India shall cooperate closely with each other on issues relating to their national interests. Neither Government shall allow the use of its territory for activities harmful to the national security and interest of the other.

Article 3

There shall, as heretofore, be free trade and commerce between the territories of the Government of Bhutan and the Government of India. Both the governments shall provide full cooperation and assistance to each other in the matter of trade and commerce.

Article 4

The Government of India agrees that the Government of Bhutan shall be free to import, from or through India into Bhutan, whatever arms, ammunition, machinery, warlike material or stores as may be required or desired for the strength and welfare of Bhutan, and that this arrangement shall hold good for all time as long as the Government of India is satisfied that the intentions of the government are friendly and that there is no danger to India from such importations. The Government of Bhutan agrees that there shall be no export of such arms, ammunition and materials outside Bhutan either by the Government of Bhutan or by private individuals.

Article 5

The Government of Bhutan and the Government of India agree that Bhutanese subjects residing in Indian territories shall have equal justice with Indian subjects, and that Indian subjects residing in Bhutan shall have equal justice with the subjects of the Government of Bhutan.

Article 6

The extradition of persons wanted by either state for crimes and for unlawful activities affecting their security shall be in keeping with the extradition agreements between the two countries.

Article 7

The Government of Bhutan and the Government of India agree to promote cultural exchanges and cooperation between the two countries. These shall be extended to such areas as education, health, sports, science and technology.

Article 8

The Government of Bhutan and the Government of India agree to continue to consolidate and expand their economic cooperation for mutual and long-term benefit.

Article 9

Any differences and disputes arising in the interpretation and application of this Treaty shall be settled bilaterally by negotiations in a spirit of trust and understanding in consonance with the historically close ties of friendship and mutually beneficial cooperation that form the bedrock of Bhutan-India relations.

Article 10

This Treaty shall come into force upon the exchange of instruments of Ratification by the two governments which take place in Thimphu within one month of the signing of this Treaty. (A press release issued by the Ministry of External Affairs on 05 March said that the instruments of Ratification having been exchanged on 02 March, the treaty had come into force with immediate effect.)

The Treaty shall continue in force in perpetuity unless terminated or modified by mutual consent.

In witness whereof, the undersigned being duly authorised thereto by their respective governments, have signed this Treaty.

Done at New Delhi on the Eighth Day of February Two Thousand and Seven, in two originals each in Hindi, Dzongkha and English languages, each text being equally authentic. However, in case of dfference, the English text shall prevail.

For the Government of For the Government of

The Republic of India the Kingdom of Bhutan

Sd/-

(Pranab Mukherjee) (H.R.H. Trongsa Penlop
Minister of External Affairs Jigme Khesar Namgyel
Wang chuck
The Crown Prince of Bhutan

Appendix 5

Statement made by His Excellency Lyonpo Dawa Tsering, Minister for Foreign Affairs of the Royal Government of Bhutan in the General Assembly of the United Nations on October 4, 1972.

Bhutan became a member of the United Nations last year. For several centuries we had followed a policy of self-imposed isolationism to preserve our country's sovereignty and independence. While the policy was successful in achieving this objective, it, however, left our country socially, economically and politically backward. The man who was primarily responsible for ending this policy and leading our country into the mainstream of the modern world was His Majesty Jigme Dorji Wangchuck, who passed away recently at the young age of forty-four years following a heart attack.

Our new King, His Majesty Jigme Singye Wangchuck, is determined to follow in the footsteps of his great father. In the sphere of foreign policy, His Majesty has reaffirmed our commitment to the ideals of the United Nations Charter and to the policy of non-alignment and friendship with all countries. In the domestic sphere, His Majesty has pledged to work selflessly and with devotion to provide our people a better, richer and a fuller life.

The preceding year has been a momentous one. Although the world continues to face many serious problems, certain hopeful signs have began to emerge. President Nixon's recent visit to China and the Soviet Union have for the first time after several decades unfolded opportunities which can usher in an era of real détente. My delegation welcomes this positive development and we hope that these new contacts which have been established between the leaders of the United States on the one hand and China and the Soviet Union on the other would contribute positively in bringing about real peace in the world. In the context of improved relations between the major powers of the world and in the context of the changes that are taking place in Asia, Africa, Latin America, Europe and other parts of the world, we can now look forward to the coming years with hope and optimism.

Mr President, for the first time in over two decades signs of peace in the Indian sub-continent have began to emerge. The possibility of a thaw in Indo-Pakistani relations is no longer a remote possibility but a possible reality which is within the grasp of the leaders of India and Pakistan. This affords the people of the sub-continent a real chance to live in peace and amity. We have noted with satisfaction the outcome of the recent summit meeting between the leaders of India and Pakistan which has resulted in some significant progress being made towards a lasting and durable peace on the sub-continent. We are convinced that the leaders of both India and Pakistan desire genuine peace and it is the hope of my government that the two countries would be to work out satisfactory solutions to their problems without interference from outside.

Bhutan welcomes the emergence of Bangladesh as an independent sovereign nation. We extended our sympathy and support to the people of Bangladesh during their struggle for national liberation and we are happy today that we were one of the first to recognise the reality of Bangladesh, a reality which has now been recognised by over ninety nations of the world. We wish the people of Bangladesh well and hope that they will be able to take their rightful place in this Assembly of nations without further delay.

The emergence of Bangladesh and the changes that are taking place in the Indian sub-continent have undoubtedly brought about new political equations in Asia. Bhutan is fully conscious of the far reaching changes that are taking place in our part of the world and we are taking the necessary steps to adjust our attitudes and policies in the context of these changes. It is gratifying to note that our relations with our neighbour, India, continue to be most cordial and friendly. Our relations with India are based on equality and mutual trust and advantage, and we look forward to an era of still greater cooperation and friendship with India in the years to come.

My delegation considers the contacts which have recently been established between the leaders of South and North Korea as a positive factor leading to the restoration of peace and normalcy in that region as a prelude to the eventual reunification of Korea. We welcome these positive developments and fully support the efforts of the people of both South and North Korea to establish durable peace in their country.

My delegation has read with great satisfaction the joint communiqué issued by the Prime Ministers of Japan and China at the conclusion of Prime Minister Tanka's visit to China. We welcome these high level contacts and the decision which was taken to normalise relations between these two great Asian countries. Improved relations between Japan and China will undoubtedly be a positive factor in ensuring peace and stability in East Asia.

We have also noted with satisfaction the climate in Europe and welcome the agreements recently signed between the Federal Republic of Germany and the Soviet Union and the Federal Republic of Germany and Poland. We also welcome the four-power agreement on Berlin and the contacts established between the Federal Republic of Germany and the German Democratic Republic with a view to improving relations between them.

These hopeful signs should not, however, blind us to the fact that the world is still not free from conflicts. In the Middle East little progress has been achieved towards a lasting peace. My delegation believes that Resolution 242 of the Security Council provides the requisite framework within which a peaceful solution of the Middle East problem could be found which would take into account the just and legitimate aspirations of all concerned. We are convinced that this problem can be solved through peaceful means without resorting to force. It is the hope of my delegation that all concerned will work towards a peaceful solution of this tragic problem.

During the last two years or so significant progress has been made in the field of disarmament.

The SALT talks between the United States and the Soviet Union have resulted in a partial accord. My delegation welcomes the recently concluded Treaty between the Soviet Union and the United States in this connection. My government is totally committed to the concept of general and complete disarmament, and would like this limited accord to be extended so as to encompass a wider area of general in all its aspects. It is in the same spirit that we welcome the agreement signed in Moscow during the visit of President Nixon relating to the joint exploration of the outer space for peaceful purposes. My delegation will continue to watch with interest the proceedings of the Conference of the Committee on Disarmament (CCD) whose achievements, though limited so far, have not been insignificant. We consider it imperative for all nuclear powers to fully participate in the deliberations of the CCD so that this forum could become more representative and effective. My delegation supports the proposal to convene, with adequate preparation, a World Disarmament Conference with the participation of all countries of the world.

Mr President, my delegation shares the concern of our distinguished Secretary-General and other governments at the alarming increase that has taken place in terrorist activities in recent months. We firmly believe that any form of intimidation or terrorist activity ought to be condemned. We view with serious concern the increase in such activities in recent years and would support any move which would, through collective action, bring an end to this senseless violence which causes suffering to so many innocent individuals.

During the last General Assembly my delegation supported the proposal to declare the Indian Ocean as a zone of peace. My government is convinced that as a first step it may be desirable to declare such areas or zones as could be mutually agreed upon as areas or zones of peace. We, however, note with regret that little progress has been made so far in implementing the provisions of the General Assembly resolution on this subject. Being a hinterland State belonging to the Indian Ocean area, Bhutan is deeply interested to ensure that the Indian Ocean and the adjoining areas should be free from becoming an area of confrontation between the super-powers.

Mr President, another area which constitutes a grave threat to international peace and security is colonialism and racialism. In spite of several years of sustained efforts of the various United Nations agencies, territories such as Angola, Mozambique, Gunea Bissau, Southern Rhodesia, and Nambia continue to be under foreign colonial occupation. My delegation is disappointed that very little progress has been made in accelerating the process of liberation of these colonial territories. My delegation has noted with regret that in spite of the pressure of world opinion the Government of South Africa continues to practice unabated policies of Apartheid and racial discrimination. My delegation also views with concern that no progress has been made to end illegal white minority rule in Southern Rhodesia. We are of the view that the hands of the Secretary-General and of the United Nations must be strengthened so that the United Nations could act as an effective instrument for ending the evils of colonialism, apartheid and racial discrimination.

Mr President, my government, like the governments of many other countries of the Third World, was disappointed at the outcome of the Third United Nations Conference on Trade and Development. If one of the major causes of friction and tension in the world has to be eliminated then we must take a determined effort to reduce the massive disparities which exist in the standard of living of the peoples of the developed and developing countries. When the General Assembly adopted the strategy for the Second United Nations Development Decade there was hope that we may yet, through collective action, solve some of the problems of trade and development. The subsequent events have, however, belied these expectations. We hope that the United Nations will be able to provide the necessary impetus and the machinery to solve these problems which are of crucial importance to the developing countries.

Mr President, during the last quarter of a century man has made remarkable strides in science and technology. Today, as we have the means to utilise this remarkable knowledge we have gained for the good of all mankind. Man is ready to explore the tremendous wealth of the space and other planets and of the seas and the oceans. The resources of the sea have a tremendous potential if harnessed properly. My government, therefore, welcomed the declaration of the principles governing the sea-bed and ocean floor and the sub-soil thereof beyond the limits of national jurisdiction adopted by the General Assembly two years ago. We continue to support all measures aimed at declaring the outer space and the sea-bed and ocean floor as the common heritage of all mankind to be reserved exclusively for peaceful purposes. My government regards the work of the Committee on the Peaceful Uses of the Sea-bed and Ocean Floor beyond the limits of National Jurisdiction as of great importance and would closely watch the outcome of the proposed Conference on the Law of the Sea scheduled to convene in 1973.

In conclusion, Mr President, I would once again like to pledge my government's continued support to the ideals and principles of the United Nations Charter. We pledge to work towards our common ideals and aspirations in the pursuit of peace. We are convinced that the United Nations remains one of the best hopes for mankind's survival. We shall not fail to contribute our modest bit in the strengthening of the United Nations so that this great organisation may continue to further the cause of world peace, progress and security.

Appendix 6

Statement made by His Excellency Mr Sangye Penjor, Permanent Representative of Bhutan to the United Nations and Head of the Delegation of Bhutan to the Fourth Summit Conference of Non-Aligned Countries on September 7, 1973.

His Majesty, the King of Bhutan, has not been able to come, I am afraid, to join this distinguished gathering.

However, it is a great pleasure and honour for me, on this historic occasion, Mr Chairman, to convey the greetings of His Majesty Jigme Singye Wangchuck, the King of Bhutan, to you, to your people and to all the distinguished leaders and delegates assembled here. It is, indeed, an honour and privilege for me to address this august body on behalf of His Majesty the King, the Government and the people of Bhutan, on the occasion of the admission of the Kingdom of Bhutan as a full member of this family of nations.

Bhutan is a landlocked country in the heart of the Himalaya with a population of slightly more than a million and has an area of 18 thousand square miles. It is perhaps one of the few countries in the world which had managed to keep away from the colonial yoke through a policy of aloofness, which was actually ended in 1962 when Bhutan became a member of the Colombo Plan for Cooperative and Economic Development in the South and Southeast Asia. In 1969, she became a member of the Universal Postal Union. Consistent with the forward looking policy, we joined the ECAPE in 1972. I would like to mention that one man who was responsible for bringing Bhutan to the international arena was His Majesty Jigme Dorji Wangchuck, the late King of Bhutan. He introduced radical political and economic changes in the country and through his wise direction of the affairs of the State, we have registered considerable progress in the economic and social fields. It is also the late King who guided the country through policy of non-alignment in external relations.

Our people today look to the new sovereign His Majesty Jigme Singye Wangchuck for guidance, comfort and inspiration. The present monarch is determined to continue the work started by his father and provide the people with a better, richer and fuller life. Our admission into this group is, therefore, another landmark in Bhutan's modern history. This will give a fresh impetus for cultivating another significant area of cordial and close relations of cooperation between countries whose foreign policy is largely shaped by the principle of non-alignment.

Our entry into this important organisation makes us all the more conscious of our need to keep in step with the developing world. Our people and the Government are fully committed to a policy of modernisation which demands change, but it is not easy to bring about change easily, when we wish to preserve our national identity, independence and sovereignty by retaining the very best in our tradition and ancient culture. However, with all our efforts geared towards this goal, we are confident of success. The country is rich in natural resources and potentials, and it is striving to develop along modern lines. The ideals Bhutan sets out to achieve is a very happy co-existence of tradition and progress. We have so far successfully completed two Five-Year Plans and have launched the Third Five-year Plan in 1971. In the process of accelerating the pace of development in the country we, indeed, have received generous economic and technical cooperation from our neighbour, India, with whom we enjoy the very best of relations. The social and economic infrastructure of the country is being built through these plans.

Mr Chairman, Bhutan is committed to the ideals of the UN Charter and its purposes and the principles of non-alignment for furthering peace and friendship with all. The full membership of Bhutan to this family of non-aligned countries, therefore, is an important occasion. It is an occasion for the fulfillment of the cherished hopes of our people. It is also an occasion for rededicating ourselves to the great principles and purposes of this Organisation. It is, therefore, appropriate to survey and review briefly the progress made in the various sectors of political and economic activities with which the non-aligned movement is concerned actively. I may state that one thing is certain, the movement with its dynamism and pragmatism in contemporary human affairs, is attracting world attention and there is an increasing number of adherents from various geographical areas of the world. This prominent feature is a reflection of the will of the large number of countries which would like to base the premises of their foreign policy on the foundations of independence of thought and action.

Today, I feel both happy and humble. Happy at the unanimous election to the full membership of this great organisation which epitomises the dreams and aspirations of the developing countries and humble as an individual who is a newcomer to this Conference and at the enormity of its tasks and oceanic depth of the understanding and cooperation it seeks today.

The Kingdom of Bhutan with its distinctive culture and tradition today embarks on a voyage of new horizons. In doing so, we not only propose to pursue the path of progress and prosperity but we also endeavour very humbly in our small way to contribute towards the success of the common efforts of the nations represented here, to achieve better and more peaceful world order. While desirous of fulfilling our role in the international relations, we have no intention of plunging into the vortex of international tensions and turmoil. Just emerging in the international arena, with our limited resources we cannot afford the luxury of getting caught in the flames of conflict. However, it is not the intention of Bhutan to shy away from playing a rightful role in the external relations on the basis of sovereign equality. Bhutan would, therefore, continue to follow a non-aligned course and a policy of peaceful co-existence, consistent with the fundamental need to increase the area of peace, reduce tensions and ensure stability with justice. It is in this spirit that we seek cooperation and security in our region.

We seek peace not only in the region but also see the need of international security. Peace and security built on a durable foundation for the benefit of all mankind in accordance with the purposes and principles of the United Nations Charter. In this connection, Bhutan welcomes the recent agreement in the Indian sub-continent between India and Pakistan with the concurrence of Bangladesh. The declaration of the Indian Ocean as a zone of peace is significant and needs to be pursued actively. There is also need to ensure that the United Nations becomes a fully effective and representative organisation for the promotion of its aims and objectives which would be in the interest of all countries. It is in this direction that Bhutan attaches importance to the universality of membership in the United Nations so that the countries still outside the United Nations could participate in the activities of the organisation. Bhutan will confirm with the non-aligned principles and will discharge all the responsibilities devolving upon us as a member. We shall also make our humble contribution to the maintenance of peace and peaceful co-existence and mutually beneficial economic cooperation. We shall support whole heartedly the aims and aspirations of the Non-Aligned Movement and work assiduously for the elimination of all forms of colonialism, racial discrimination and apartheid and join hands with all the members of the Group.

The Security Council a few months back considered vigorously the situation in the Middle East but the debate unfortunately has not brought us any nearer to a peaceful solution. In fact, the situation continues to constitute a violation of the United Nations principles, a challenge to the aims of Non-Aligned countries and a grave threat to peace. However, we must hope for peace in that region. It is this hope and the United Nations Security Resolution 242 which we believe still provide a good basis for peace in the Middle East.

Last, but not the least, is the concern of all the developing countries to exercise complete sovereignty over their natural resources, the importance of which in the pursuit of economic development need not be over-emphasised here. The natural resources form the backbone of the economic development efforts in most of the developing countries. Today, with all the lofty aims of the international development strategy, disappointing trends are becoming evident in the Second UN Development Decade Programme.

The gap between the developed and the developing countries is widening. This shows that efforts at national and international levels have fallen short of the target set out in the international development strategy. This is particularly obvious in the implementation of the special measures in favour of the least developed and also land-locked countries. The geographically handicapped countries are in greater need of attention. My country will support all measures to be adopted at this Summit for accelerating the economic development of the developing countries. My delegation sincerely hopes that at the forthcoming Law of the Sea Conference, the non-aligned group acting in harmony will understand and safeguard the legitimate needs of the land-locked countries.

Before I conclude, Mr Chairman, I would like to reaffirm that Bhutan would adhere to the principles and objectives of the policy of non-alignment for ensuring peaceful co-existence and friendship with all. We believe in freedom, freedom for the people of each country, to follow their destiny without external interference and above all, we believe in the dignity of man as an individual whatever his race, colour or creed, and his right to a better, fuller and richer life.

Appendix 7

Address of His Majesty Jigme Singye Wangchuck, King of Bhutan to the First SAARC Summit Meeting, Dhaka, 7-8 December 1985.

Mr Chairman,

May I begin by congratulating you warmly on your unanimous election as Chairman of the first summit meeting of South Asian countries? This meeting is an occasion of historic significance for our region, manifesting our united commitment to regional peace, cooperation, and advancement. Mr Chairman, along with the high distinction conferred upon you, the nations gathered here today have placed upon your shoulders the heavy responsibility of guiding our regional body for the next two years. For our part, we pledge our whole-hearted support to you in furthering the noble objectives of SAARC.

Mr Chairman, I would like to say how happy I am that this meeting is taking place in the capital of a country with which we have extremely close ties of friendship and cooperation. The fact that this meeting is taking place in Dhaka is a recognition of the vital role that Bangladesh has played in the formative stage of SARC and an indication of the confidence we have in your wisdom and ability to lead our regional organisation. I would also like to express our deep gratitude to you and your people for the excellent arrangements made for this meeting, and for the warm reception and generous hospitality accorded to me and the members of my delegation.

As we embark on our voyage of regional integration and unity, we wish to pay tribute to two distinguished leaders who made a lasting contribution to SAARC and who are no more with us. The late President Zia-ur Rahman of Bangladesh pioneered the concept of SAARC, and the Prime Minister Indira Gandhi of India lent her firm and unwavering support to this endeavour in its crucial period.

After five years of gradual and painstaking labour our efforts to build regional cooperation in South Asia have culminated in this summit. As we meet here over the next two days, we will initiate the process of creating a climate of peace and cooperation in our region, based on mutual understanding, goodwill, and trust. This process will not be easy, given our political and strategic divergences and asymmetries in our sizes, resources, and levels of development. On the other hand, we must bear in mind that in spite of all our heterogeneity we are geographically one homogeneous unit, that our peoples have lived together in peace and friendship for countless centuries, and that they share many values rooted in our common past.

Mr Chairman, it may neither be possible nor desirable to limit discussions in our meetings to issues of a non-political nature, for the political climate of our region will undoubtedly cast a long shadow over our deliberations. In the geographical realities of our region, it would be unrealistic to ignore the primacy of the political factor, as, in the final analysis, it will be the political environment of the region which will determine the shape and scope of regional cooperation in South Asia. The main obstacle to be overcome is not only the psychological and emotional barriers of the past, but the fears, anxieties, and apprehensions of the present. If regional cooperation is to be enhanced we have to move away from an attitude of suspicion to one of understanding and trust despite major differences in political and security perceptions. We must transcend the narrow nationalism that prevails in our region due largely to historical reasons and create good neighbourly relationship in which the magnanimity of the larger states would be matched by the genuine friendship of the smaller states.

Mr Chairman, in our deep concern over global military expenditure and the escalating arms race, we are heartened and encouraged by the recent summit in Geneva between the leaders of the two Super Powers. We would like to express the hope that this initiative will gain momentum and substance through a continued process towards gradual nuclear disarmament.

In our own region it is regrettable to note that the arms race has intensified and assumed new dimensions with the increasing possibility of the development of nuclear weapons. While we stand united in our call for general and complete disarmament in the global context, it is a political reality that this ominous development in our region can be effectively resolved only through a meaningful dialogue between the countries concerned. At the same time, we are firm in our belief that SAARC can and must play a determining role in furthering better and closer understanding within the region in order to create an atmosphere conducive to amicable settlement of differences.

South Asia is the cradle of one of the earliest human civilizations. We are all heirs to glorious spiritual and cultural traditions. Yet, today, in terms of social and economic wellbeing, the situation in our region could not be more dismal. The region's one billion people, representing one-fifth of mankind, live on 3.3 per cent of the global land area with a per capita income of less than one-tenth of the world's average. While the rate of economic growth is low as against a high rate of population increase, nearly half of our peoples live in absolute poverty. In this unhappy situation, regional cooperation with stress on self-reliance, offers a viable alternative development strategy. In our view, collective self-reliance and independence through interdependence within the framework of regional cooperation is not only desirable but imperative in the face of the present global realities.

The current international environment which has placed severe strains on our national economies favours the regional option and greater South-South cooperation. At the same time, we must persist in our efforts to establish the New International Economic Order. A congruity of views regarding international economics and North-South relations already exists among our countries. What is now required is coordination and harmonisation of our policies on the internal economic front through our regional organisation. Once regional cooperation succeeds in producing visible economic gains and a climate of trust is developed, the scope for mutually beneficial economic cooperation would expand. In this respect, the establishment of an Integrated Programme of Action in nine areas of direct benefit to all our peoples is a noteworthy achievement. However, progress in establishing cooperative linkages in some areas has been rather slow. I am confident that this summit meeting will provide the necessary impetus to cooperation in these areas.

The Kingdom of Bhutan has been a firm and consistent supporter of the concept of regional cooperation from the very beginning. It is our conviction that a vital factor in this endeavour is the determined commitment and support of all our seven nations to the principles and objectives of SAARC which are based on sovereign equality, peaceful co-existence, and mutual benefit. The common hopes and aspirations of our peoples which have brought us together on this occasion can best be fulfilled through the exercise of wisdom, vision, and political will at the summit level. We believe that it will be the personal and unwavering commitment of the leaders themselves that will determine the outcome of this summit and the future course of regional cooperation. It is in this context that we welcome the proposal to establish the South Asian Association for Regional Cooperation and we pledge our full support to this body.

Mr Chairman, in conclusion, I would like to express my fervent hope that future generations will find reasons to look back on this historic summit as the beginning of a new era in inter-state relations in South Asia, and heralding the dawn of regional peace, meaningful cooperation, genuine friendship and mutual prosperity.

I wish you all Tashi Delek !

Bibliography

Government Documents and Publications

1. Political Missions to Bhutan, comprising the Reports of Ashley Eden, 1864, R. B. Pemberton, 1838, with Dr.W. Grifith's Journal, and the account by Kishan Kant Bose, Calcutta, 1865.
2. Statistical Yearbook of Bhutan, Thimphu, 1991.
3. Ninth Five Year Plan: Main document, Thimphu, 2002.
4. Bhutan's policy statements in the UN, Non-aligned meetings, SAARC and BIMSTEC Summits.
5. Bhutan in focus, Royal Bhutanese Embassy, New Delhi, 2003.
6. The Constitution of The Kingdom of Bhutan, Thimphu, 2005.
7. Kuensel (A Weekly official bulletin of the Royal Government of Bhutan. However, in the 1980s Kuensel was made National Newspaper of Bhutan).
8. IDA-Bhutan: Website.

Books

Abrol, Mridula, British Relations with Frontier States, New Delhi, 1974.

Aleaz, Bonita and Ghosh, Lipi and Dutta, Achintya Kumar, ed., Ethnicity, Nations and Minorities: The South Asian Scenario, New Delhi, 2003.

Appadorai, A. and Rajan, M.S., India's Foreign Policy and Relations, New Delhi, 1985.

Aris, Michael, Bhutan: The Early History of a Himalayan Kingdom, New Delhi, 1980.

——————, Views of Medieval Bhutan: The Diary and Drawings of Samuel Davis, 1783, London, New Delhi, 1982.

Bajpai, U.S., ed., India and its Neighbourhood, New Delhi, 1986.

Banerjee, A. C., The Eastern Frontier of British India, 1784-1826, Calcutta, 1946.

Bell, Charles, Tibet: Past and Present, Oxford, 1924.

Bhuyan, S. K., Ango-Assamese Relations, 1771-1826, Gauhati, 1949.

Bhasin, Avtar Singh, ed., India's Foreign Relations-2007: Documents, New Delhi, 2008.

Bandyopadhyaya, Jayantanuja, Making of India's foreign policy: Determinants, institutions, processes and personalities, New Delhi, 1980.

Brecher, Michael, The New States of Asia: A Political Analysis, London, 1969.

Chakravarti, P. C., India-China Relations, Calcutta, 1961.

Chakravarty, S. R., ed., Foreign Policy of Bangladesh, New Delhi, 1994.

Coelho, V. H., Sikkim and Bhutan, New Delhi, 1967.

Darbar, Gyanvati, Portrait of a President: Letters of Dr. Rajendra Prasad, New Delhi, 1976.

Das, B. S., Mission to Bhutan: A Nation in Transition, New Delhi, 1995.

Das, Nirmala, The Dragon Country, New Delhi, 1973.

Deb, Arbinda, Bhutan and India: A Study in Frontier Political Relations, Calcutta, 1976.

Dharamadasani, M. D. ed., Contemporary South Asia, Varanasi, 1985.

————, Politics and Economy of Bhutan, Varanasi, N. D.

Doji, Dasho Rigzin, A Brief Religious, Cultural and Secular History of Bhutan, New York, 1989.

Dutt, V. P., India's Foreign Policy, New Delhi, 1984.

Frankel, Joseph, International Relations in a changing World, Oxford, 1979.

Gellner, E., Nation and Nationalism, Oxford, 1983.

Ghose, Partha S., Cooperation and Conflict in South Asia, New Delhi, 1989.

Gopal, S., British Policy in India, 1858-1905, Cambridge, 1965.

————, ed., Selected Works of Jawaharlal Nehru, New Delhi, 1987.

Goyal, N., Political History of the Himalayan States, New Delhi, 1966.

Gupta, Shantiswarup, British Relations With Bhutan, Jaipur, 1074.

Hafiz, M. Abul and Khan, Abur Rob, ed., Security of Small States, Dhaka, 1987.

Hasrat, Bikramajit, History of Bhutan: Land of the Peaceful Dragon, Thimphu, 1980.

Huntington, Samuel P., Political Order in Changing Societies, New Haven, 1970.

Iftekharuzzyaman, M. A. H., ed., South Asian Regional Cooperation: A Socio-economic Approach to Peace and Stability, Dhaka, 1985.

Jetly, Nancy, ed., Regional Security in South Asia: The Ethno-Sectarian Dimensions, New Delhi, 1999.

Karan, Pradyumna P., and Jenkins Jr. William M., The Himalayan Kingdoms: Bhutan, Sikkim and Nepal, Princeton, 1963.

————, Bhutan: A Physical and Cultural Geography, Lexington, 1967.

Kodikara, Shelton U., Strategic Factors in Inter-State Relations in South Asia, Delhi, 1984.

Kohli, Manorama, India and Bhutan: A Study in Interrelations,1772-1910, New Delhi, 1982.

————, From Dependency to Interdependence: A Study of Indo-Bhutan Relations, New Delhi, 1993.

Kyi, Aung San Sun, Let's Visit Bhutan, London, 1985.

Lamb, Alastair, Britain and Chinese Central Asia: The Road to Lhasa, 1767-1905, London, 1960.

Labh, Kapileshwar, India and Bhutan, New Delhi, 1974.

Macridis, Roy C., ed., Foreign Policy in World Politics, New Jersey, 1972.

Mehra, G. N., Bhutan: Land of the Peaceful Dragon, Delhi, 1974.

Mehra P., The Younghusband Expedition: An Interpretation, Bombay, 1968.

Menon, K. P. S., China: Past and Present, Bombay, 1968.

Misra, R. C., Emergence of Bhutan, Jaipur, 1989.

Misra, K.P. and Narayanan, K. R., ed., Non-Alignment in Contemporary International Relations, Delhi, 1981.

Modelsky, George, A Theory of Foreign Policy, New York, 1967.

Morgenthau, Hans J., Politics Among Nations: The Struggle for Power and Peace, New York, 1963.

Muni, S. D., Foreign Policy of Nepal, New Delhi, 1970.

Muni, S. D. and Muni, Anuradha, Regional Cooperation in South Asia, New Delhi, 1984.

Muni, S. D. and Baral, Lok Raj, ed., Refugees and Regional Security in South Asia, Delhi, 1996.

Narain, Virendra and Upreti, B. C., ed., SAARC: A Study of Perceptions and Policies, New Delhi, 1991.

Nehru, Jawaharlal, India's Foreign Policy: Selected Speeches, September 1946—April 1961, Delhi, 1961.

Noorani, A. G., India, the Superpowers and the neighbours: Essays in foreign policy, New Delhi, 1985.

Panikkar, K. M., Asia and Western Dominance: A Survey of the Vasco De Gama epoch of Asian History, 1498-1945, London, 1953.

Parmanand, Political Development in South Asia, New Delhi, 1988.

————, The Politics of Bhutan: Retrospect and Prospect, Delhi, 1992.

Phadnis, Urmila, Ethnicity and Nation-Building in South Asia, New Delhi, 1990.

Pemberton, R. B., Political Mission to Bhutan, Calcutta, 1865.

Phadnis, Urmila, Muni, S. D. and Bahadur, Kalim, ed., Domestic Conflicts in South Asia, New Delhi, 1986.

Pommaret, Francoise, An Illustrated Guide to Bhutan, Hong Kong, 1990.

Prasad, B., The Foundation of India's Foreign Policy, Calcutta, 1955.

Prasad, Bimal, The Origins of Indian Foreign Policy, Calcutta, 1960.

————, ed., India's Foreign Policy: Studies in Continuity and Change, New Delhi, 1978.

————, ed., Regional Cooperation in South Asia: Problems and Prospects, New Delhi, 1988.

Rahul, Ram, Modern Bhutan, Delhi, 1971.

————, Royal Bhutan, New Delhi, 1983.

————, The Rise of Nepal and Bhutan, New Delhi, 1984.

Ramakant, Indo-Nepalese Relations, 1816-1877, Delhi, 1968.

Ramakant and Misra, R. C., ed., Bhutan: Society and Polity, New Delhi, 1996.

Rasgotra, M., Chopra, V. D. and Misra, K. P., ed., India's Foreign Policy in the 1990s, New Delhi, 1990.

Rathore, Laxman Singh, The Changing Bhutan, New Delhi, 1974.

Rennie, Surgeon, Bootan and the Story of the Dooar War, London, 1866.

Richardson, H. E., Tibet and its History, London, 1962.

Ronaldshay, Earl of Lands of the Thunderbolt, London, 1923.

Rose, Leo E., The Politics of Bhutan, New York, 1977.

Rosenau, James N., ed., Linkage Politics: Essays on the convergence of National and International Systems, New York, 1963.

————, Domestic Sources of Foreign Policy, New York, 1967.

Rothstein, Robert L., Alliances and Small Powers, New York, 1968.

Rustomji, Nari, Bhutan: The Dragon Kingdom in Crisis, Oxford, 1978.

Sanskrityayan, Kamala, Bhutan: The Land and People, Delhi, 1971.

Sen Gupta, Bhabani, Bhutan: Towards a Grass-root Participatory Polity, New Delhi, 1999.

Shakabpa, Tsepon W. D., Tibet: A Political History, London, 1967.

Singh, Nagendra, Bhutan: A Kingdom in the Himalayas, New Delhi, 1972.

Sinha, A. C., Bhutan: Ethnic Identity and National Dilemma, New Delhi, 1991 and 1993.

Varma, Shanti Prasad, Struggle for the Himalayas: A Study in Sino-Indian Relations, New Delhi, 1971.

Varma, S. P. and Misra, K. P., ed., Foreign Policies in South Asia, New Delhi, 1969.

Verma, Ravi, India's Role in the Emergence of Contemporary Bhutan, Delhi, 1988.

Vital, David, The Survival of Small States: Studies in Small Power—Great Power Conflict, London, 1971.

————, The Inequality of States: A Study of Small Power in International Relations, London, 1972.

White, J. C., Sikkim and Bhutan: Twenty-one Years on the North-East Frontier, 1887-1908, London, 1909.

Articles

Anil, R. N., "The Kings of Bhutan", Hindustan Times, New Delhi, 21 February 1985.

———, "Bhutan's Dilemma", Unity International, Vol. 15, No. 4, New Delhi, April 1991.

Bailey, F. M., "Travel in Bhutan", Journal of the Central Asian Society, Vol. 17, April 1930, pp. 206-20.

Belfigalio, J. Valentine, "India's Economic and Political Relations with Bhutan", Asian Survey, Vol. 12, No. 8, August 1972, pp. 676-86.

Bell, Charles, "The North-Eastern Frontier of India", Journal of the Central Asian Society, Vol. 17, April 1930, pp. 221-5.

Bhattacharya, S. S., "Bhutan in the Early Ages", the Indian History Congress, Allahabad, December 1965.

———, "Bhutan Towards Modernisation", in Ramakant and Misra, R. C., ed., Bhutan: Society and Polity, New Delhi, 1996, pp. 137-56.

Bhola, P. L., "Bhutan—Pakistan Relations," in Ramakant and Misra, R. C., ed., *op.cit.*, pp. 309-20.

Datta-Ray, Sunanda K., "Druk Past & Present—1 : Catching Up With The 20th Century", The Statesman, 10 July 1983.

———, "Druk Past and Present—11: Strategies For Survival", *Ibid.*, 11 July 1983.

———, "Flight of The Dragon—1: Bhutan's Three –Pronged Strategy", *Ibid.*, 27 April 1984.

———, "Flight of The Dragon—11: Challenge of Settlement With China", *Ibid.*, 28 April 1984.

Dharamdhasani, M. D. "Economic Development and Modernization in Bhutan", in Ramakant and Misra. R. C. ed., Bhutan: Society and Polity, New Delhi, 1996, pp. 195-203.

Dutt, Srikant, "Bhutan's International Position", International Studies, Vol. 20, Nos. 3-4, New Delhi, July-December 1981, pp. 601-23.

Ghosh, Manash, "Bhutan's survival at stake: Tsering", (an interview with Foreign Minister Dawa Tsering), The Sunday Statesman, 26 June 1992.

Gupta, S. S., "Indo-Bhutan Relations", in Ramakant and Misra, R. C., ed., Bhutan: Society and Polity, New Delhi, 1996, pp. 292-99.

Joseph, C., Mathew, " Political Economy of Ethnic Conflict in Bhutan," in Ramakant and Misra, R. C., ed., *op. cit.* pp. 116-33.

Karan, Pradyumna P., "Geo-political Structure of Bhutan," India Quarterly, Vol. 19, No. 3, July-September 1963, pp. 203-13.

Khanna, Vinod C., "Indo-Bhutan Relations in the Changing South Asian Context", in Ramakant and Misra , R. C. , ed., *op. cit.,* pp. 300-08.

Kohli, Manorama, " Dragon Kingdom's Urge For An International Role", India Quarterly, Vol. 37, No. 2, April-June 1981, pp. 227-49.

————, "Chinese Interest In Bhutan: Evolution of the British Indian Perspective," China Report, Vol. 19, No. 4, July-August 1983, pp. 37-46.

————, "Bhutan's Strategic Environment: Changing Perceptions", India Quartely, Vol. 42, No. 2, New Delhi, April-June 1986, pp. 142-53.

————, "Ethnic Crisis in Bhutan: Implications," in Ramakant and Misra, R. C., ed., *op. cit.,* pp. 92-99.

Kumara, D. P., "Appeal to Bhutan terrorists," The Statesman, 14 October 1990.

————, "Fear still haunts South Bhutan," *Ibid.,* 18 October 1990.

Labh, Kapileshwar, "The International Status of Bhutan Before 1947," International Studies, January-March 1974, New Delhi, pp. 75-93.

————, "The Himalayan Kingdom of Bhutan; Issues and Trends," in M. D. Dharamdasani, ed., Contemporary South Asia, Varanasi, 1985, pp.138-49.

————, "The Himalayan Frontier: A Case Study of the Bhutanese Part of the Frontier," in N. R. Ray, ed., Himalayan Frontier in Historical Perspectives, Calcutta, 1986, pp. 388-99.

————, "Monarchical System of Bhutan: Challenges of Modernization," in UrmilaPhadnis, S. D. Muni and KalimBahadur, ed., Domestic Conflicts in South Asia: Economic and Ethnic Dimensions, Vol. 2, New Delhi, 1986, pp.182-95.

————, "Bhutan and SAARC," in Virendra Narain and B. C. Upreti, ed., SAARC: A Study of Perceptions and Policies, New Delhi, 1986, pp. 125-35.

————, "Dakshes—Sanghke Sadsyonke Beech Aarthik Sahayog: Samsyayen Aur Samsyayen" (Economic Cooperation among SAARC members: Problems and Prospects), Samyik Samajik Chintan, Indian Academy of Social Sciences, Allahabad, 1992, pp. 33-52.

————, "Bhutan: Ethnic Problems Evade Solutions," Himalaya Today, March-August 1993, pp. 19-22.

————, "Economic Development in Bhutan: Recent Trends and Prospects," International Studies, Vol. 31, No. 2, April-June 1994, pp. 189-206.

————, "Bangladesh—Bhutan Partnership in Peace and Economic Development: Commonalities and Constraints," in S. R. Chakravarty, ed., Foreign Policy of Bangladesh, New Delhi, 1994, pp. 232-43.

————, "Ethnic Factor in the Himalayan Kingdoms," International Studies, Vol. 32, No. 3, July-September 1995, pp. 283-95.

————, "Political Development of Bhutan: Emerging Trends," in Ramakant and Misra, R. C., ed., *op. cit.,* pp. 207-17.

————, "Ethnic Resurgence in the Himalayan States of Nepal and Bhutan," in Nancy Jetly, ed.., Regional Security in South Asia: The Ethnic—Sectarian Dimensions, New Delhi, 1999.

————, "Bhutan's Initiatives in Domestic and Foreign Spheres," in M. D. Dharamdasani, ed., Politics and Economy of Bhutan, Varanasi, N. D.. pp. 1-17.

————, "Minority And Identity Questions In Bhutan," in Bonita Aleaz, Lipi Ghose and Achintya Kumar Dutta, ed., Ethnicity, Nations and Minorities: The South Asian Scenario, New Delhi, 2003, pp. 61-73.

Lama, Mahendra P., "Bhutan: A Changing Development Paradigm," in Ramakant and Misra, R. C. , ed., *op. cit.,* pp. 157-65.

Mehrotra, Smita, "Economic Development in Bhutan: Recent Trends," in Ramakant and Misra, R. C., ed., *op. cit.,* pp.186-94.

Misra, Meenakshi and Misra, R. C., "Bhutan's Foreign Policy in the New Context," in Ramakant and Misra, R. C., ed., *op. cit.,* pp. 274-84.

Misra, R.C., "Bhutan-China Relations," China Report, Vol. 17, No. 2, March-April 1981, pp. 43-50.

————, "Tibetans in Bhutan: Problem of Repatriation," China Report, Vol. 18, No. 5, September-October 1982, pp. 25-32.

Nanda, Prakash, "Foreign Affairs: Is Bhutan likely to do a Nepal on India ?" Times of India, New Delhi, 11 May 1989.

Narayan, Hemendra, "Bhutanese refugees in Nepal: Caught between frying pan and fire," Indian Express, New Delhi, 19 February 1992.

Palmer, Norman D., "Trans-Himalayan Confrontation," Orbis, Vol. 6, No. 4, Winter 1963, pp. 513-27.

Parmanand, "Indo-Bhutan Relations in the Nineties," in Rasgotra, M., Chopra, V.D., and Misra, K. P., ed., India's Foreign Policy in the 1990s, New Delhi, 1990, pp. 325-37.

————, "India-Bhutan Friendship and Bhutan's Problem of National Integration," Strategic Analysis, Vol. 13, No. 12, New Delhi, March 1991, pp.1411-24.

————, "Bhutan: Phoney Crisis of Integration," Times of India, New Delhi, 20 November 1991.

————, "Bhutan's Problem of Ethnicity: Causes, Consequences and Prospects," in Ramakant and Misra, R. C., ed., *op. cit.*, pp. 100-15.

Poulose, T. T., "Bhutan's External Relations and India," The International and Comparative Law Quarterly, London, April 1971, pp. 195-212.

Rabgye, SonamT., "Current developments in Bhutan and its implications," Unity International, Vol. 15, No. 4, April 1991, pp. 7-8.

————, "Indo-Bhutan Relations," in Ramakant and Misra, R.C., ed., *op. cit.*, pp. 285-91.

Rahul, Ram, "Making of Modern Bhutan," International Studies, Vol. 19, No. 3. July-September 1980, pp. 515-28.

Rattan, Kamaljeet, "Bhutan: Between two Worlds," India Today, 15 September 1980, pp.134-37.

Rose, Leo E., "Sino-Indian Rivalry and the Himalayan Border States," Orbis, Vol. 5, No.2, Summer 1961, pp. 198-215.

Roychoudhary, Tapash K. , "Indians' Settlements in Bhutan: Their History and Problems," in Singh, I. J. Bahadur, ed., Indians in the South Asia, New Delhi, 1984, pp.125-35.

Sarcar, S.C. , "Some Notes on the Intercourse of Bengal with the Northern Countries in the second half of the Eighteenth Century," Bengal Past and Present, Vol. 41, No. 82, April-June 1931, pp.119-27.

Sen Gupta, Bhabani, "Bhutan: Slow, steady pace of change," Hindustan Times, New Delhi, 08 January 1988.

Sharma, L. K., "No diplomatic ties with China-Bhutan," Times of India, New Delhi, 16 May 1985.

Sriram, K., "India, Bhutan for world peace," Indian Express, New Delhi, 30 September 1985.

Thinley, DashoJigmi, "Current Situation in Bhutan," in Ramakant and Misra, R. C., ed., *op.cit.,* pp. 218-61.

Upadhyay, Shashi, "Bhutan and SAARC," in Ramakant and Misra, R.C., ed., op. cit., pp. 321-27.

Upreti, B. C., "The Nepali Immigrants in Bhutan: Growing Conflict Between National and Ethnic Identities," in Ramakant and Misra, R. C., ed., *op. cit.,* pp.78-91.

Zimba, Dasho Yeshey, "Bhutan: Three Decades of Planned Development," in Ramakant and Misra, R. C., ed., *op. cit.*, pp. 166-85.

Index